Business PLUS

Preparing for the workplace

Margaret Helliwell

CAMBRIDGE
UNIVERSITY PRESS

Student's Book 3

CAMBRIDGE
UNIVERSITY PRESS

University Printing House, Cambridge CB2 8BS, United Kingdom

One Liberty Plaza, 20th Floor, New York, NY 10006, USA

477 Williamstown Road, Port Melbourne, VIC 3207, Australia

4843/24, 2nd Floor, Ansari Road, Daryaganj, Delhi – 110002, India

79 Anson Road, #06–04/06, Singapore 079906

Cambridge University Press is part of the University of Cambridge.

It furthers the University's mission by disseminating knowledge in the pursuit of education, learning and research at the highest international levels of excellence.

www.cambridge.org
Information on this title: www.cambridge.org/9781107661875

First published 2015
20 19 18 17 16 15 14 13 12 11 10 9 8 7 6 5 4 3

Printed in Malaysia by Vivar Printing

ISBN 978-1-107-66187-5 paperback Student's Book 3
ISBN 978-1-107-66886-7 paperback Teacher's Manual 3

Additional resources for this publication at www.cambridge.org/businessplus

Cambridge University Press has no responsibility for the persistence or accuracy of URLs for external or third-party internet websites referred to in this publication, and does not guarantee that any content on such websites is, or will remain, accurate or appropriate. Information regarding prices, travel timetables, and other factual information given in this work is correct at the time of first printing but Cambridge University Press does not guarantee the accuracy of such information thereafter.

Acknowledgments

The author and publisher thank the many teachers in the Asian region whose invaluable insights helped revise and fine-tune *Business Plus*. We would like to mention the following in particular:

Professor Hyojin Chung, Dongguk University, South Korea

Da-Fu Huang, Southern Taiwan University of Science and Technology, Tainan, Taiwan

Hsiu-Hui Su, Chaoyang University of Technology, Taichung, Taiwan

Gideon Hockley-Hills, SEICO Inc., Osaka, Japan

Kelly Kimura, Soka University, Tokyo, Japan

Ms. Sirirat Poomprasart, University of the Thai Chamber of Commerce (UTCC), Bangkok, Thailand

The author's special thanks go out to Stuart Vinnie, Cambridge University Press Senior Development Manager, Asia, whose experience of teachers' needs and teaching situations throughout Asia helped to mold her materials to best match the reality in the classroom, and on the editorial side, Chris Caridia, for his good ideas and endless patience. Last but not least, Bob Culverhouse and Ann Jobson for hours of patient listening!

The author would also like to thank the following Cambridge University Press regional staff for their support and advice, without which this course would never have been possible: Nuntaporn Phromphruk, Panthipa Rojanasuworapong and Sura Suksingh (Thailand); Ron Kim and Seil Choi (South Korea); Tomomi Katsuki, John Letcher, and David Moser (Japan); Irene Yang (Taiwan).

Book and cover design by Designers Collective
Book layout by Transnet Pte Ltd
Illustrations by Albert Design House
Casting and audio production by Andovar

Plan of the book

Reading	Culture focus	Business writing	Learning outcomes
			Students can . . .
The wedding planners	Who works the hardest?		▪ understand a conversation and talk about time management. ▪ make wishes about the present. ▪ use expressions with *It's* + adjective + infinitive. ▪ understand an interview about escaping from the digital world. ▪ talk about time and money, using words that go together. ▪ understand an article about wedding tourism. ▪ talk about work hours in different countries.
Door-to-door		Placing an order	▪ understand people talking about the services they provide. ▪ use the forms *get/have something done*. ▪ use *little*, *less*, *least* and *few*, *fewer*, *fewest*. ▪ understand a call center conversation. ▪ talk about successful franchise companies. ▪ talk about different jobs in the service industry. ▪ give, receive, and check information. ▪ understand an article about Japanese delivery services. ▪ understand and write a purchase order.
Lucky or unlucky?	Gift-giving customs and etiquette		▪ understand some basic marketing ideas. ▪ use the gerund as subject or object and after prepositions. ▪ use definite and indefinite articles. ▪ understand a conversation and talk about brands and logos. ▪ use a lot of different marketing words. ▪ stress the correct syllable in different words. ▪ understand an article about lucky and unlucky numbers and colors. ▪ understand and talk about gift-giving customs.
Job (dis)satisfaction		Summaries and reports	▪ understand and talk about problems at work. ▪ use reported speech in statements. ▪ use the past continuous. ▪ understand some of the problems of a foreign boss. ▪ talk about solving conflicts. ▪ use two- and three-word phrasal verbs. ▪ make nouns and adjectives by using suffixes. ▪ understand an article about job satisfaction. ▪ understand how to write summaries and reports.
Speak like an American	Business cultures		▪ understand a conversation about communication media. ▪ talk about past events using the past perfect. ▪ use the present and past tenses. ▪ listen to and summarize business news stories. ▪ use compound nouns and adjectives. ▪ ask for and give opinions, agree and disagree. ▪ understand an article about English accents. ▪ understand some differences between business cultures.

Plan of the book

Before you begin

Can you match the business situations in Units 1–10 with the photos? Then check the units.

1 **Planning and organizing**
Getting organized

2 **Service industries**
Service providers

3 **Marketing**
The four *P*s

4 **Problems and conflicts**
Problems at work

5 **Getting your message across**
Communication media

6 **Meetings and discussions**
Planning an international conference

7 **Presentations**
The dos and don'ts of presentations

8 **The world of work**
Different types of work

9 **Business and the environment**
How green is your office?

10 **Finding a job**
Job hunting

Planning and organizing

1 Business situation
Getting organized

A 🔊 **1** Lee Ji-yun works for an international company in Seoul. She is talking to her American co-workers Scott and Ted about time management. Listen to their conversation. Who says what? Write *J* for Ji-yun, *S* for Scott, and *T* for Ted.

1 You're good at time management.   *S*
2 You put in extra time nearly every weekend.   ....
3 I make to-do lists.   ....
4 It's helpful to make a daily list.   ....
5 I wish I had more free time.   ....
6 I'm way behind schedule.   ....
7 It's necessary (. . .) to set priorities.   ....

B 🔊 **1** Listen to the conversation again and answer the questions.

1 What does Scott find it difficult to do?
2 How does Ted manage his time?
3 Why does Scott think to-do lists are a waste of time?
4 What does Ji-yun's daily to-do list help her to do?
5 Why does Scott do unimportant tasks first?
6 What will Ted and Ji-yun do to help Scott?

C Work with a partner. Take turns to ask and answer the questions.

1 How do you organize your time and remember your appointments? Do you use your phone, sticky notes, or something else? Do you make to-do lists? Why or why not?
2 Are you more like Scott or like Ted in your time management? Give reasons.

▷ ▪ deadline ▪ time management
    ▪ priority ▪ to keep track

I can understand a conversation about time management.

A 🔊 **1** Listen to the conversation in 1A again and complete Scott's wishes.

Facts about Scott	Scott's wishes
Scott *doesn't have* much free time.	He wishes he .... more free time.
He *gets* stressed out.	He wishes he .... stressed out.
He *is* not well organized.	He wishes he .... better organized.
There *are* not enough hours in the day.	He wishes there .... more hours in a day.

Complete the rule.

We use *wish* + the .... tense to express wishes about the present.

With *to be*, we can use *was* or *were* for singular nouns and pronouns:
I wish I was / were better organized.

B Read the facts and complete the sentences.

1 I don't have time to relax. I wish *I had time to relax.*
2 Scott isn't good at time management. He wishes ....
3 I'm behind schedule. I wish ....
4 Ji-yun and Ted can't help Scott. They wish ....
5 Scott has to put in extra time. He wishes ....
6 Ji-yun doesn't know the answer. She wishes ....
7 I sometimes miss my deadlines. I wish ....
8 Scott's boss always says that time is money. Scott wishes his boss ....

C Work with a partner. Take turns to ask and answer the questions.

1 Where do you wish you were right now?
2 Which three things do you wish you owned?
3 What do you wish you could spend more time doing?
4 What do you wish you could spend less time doing?
5 Which talent do you wish you had?
6 Which famous person do you wish you could meet? Why?

I wish it was Friday.

▷ ▪ on schedule ▪ behind schedule
▪ quality of life

I can make wishes about the present.

Grammar focus
Focus 2: *It's* + adjective + infinitive

D Read the transcript for the conversation in 1A on page 95. Check (✔) the phrases you can find. Then complete the rule.

☐ It's difficult to . . .   ☐ It's helpful to . . .
☐ It's important to . . .   ☐ It's not good to . . .
☐ It's not hard to . . .   ☐ It's necessary to . . .
☐ It's not easy to . . .   ☐ It's useful to . . .

It's + an adjective is followed by the . . . . form of the verb.

We can also use some nouns with *It's . . .* :
It's a good idea to make a to-do list.
It's a difficult question to answer.

E Use *It's . . . to* with the words or phrases in the box to complete the sentences. Use each word/phrase only once. Compare your ideas with a partner.

| a good idea | difficult | good | important |
| not a good idea | not easy | not nice | ~~unhelpful~~ |

1 . . . argue with your co-workers.
    It's unhelpful to argue with your co-workers.
2 . . . apologize when you have done something wrong.
3 . . . learn a foreign language.
4 . . . find time to relax after work.
5 . . . hear that you are well again.
6 . . . manage your time well.
7 . . . say unkind things about other people.
8 . . . miss your deadlines.

It's not a good idea to shout at your co-workers.

F Make sentences with your own ideas. Compare your ideas with a partner.

1 It's dangerous to . . .
2 It's not easy to . . .
3 It's expensive to . . .
4 It's interesting to . . .
5 It's not hard to . . .
6 It's a good idea to . . .
7 It's impossible to . . .
8 It's not expensive to . . .

DANGER!

G Work with a partner. Make a list of tips for a good relationship between classmates or friends. Three tips should be with *not* and three tips without *not*.

It's not helpful to criticize a friend's ideas.
It's important to discuss things together.

I can use expressions with It's + adjective + infinitive.

A [2] **Listen to an interview with Japanese businessman Takumi Ito and answer the questions.**

1 What does work-life balance mean?
2 Why does Takumi need a place to escape?
3 Name four things that Takumi does in his "escape room."
4 Name three pieces of furniture in the room.
5 What effect has the escape room had on Takumi?

B [2] **Listen to the interview again. Check (✔) true, false, or not stated. Correct the false statements.**

	True	False	Not stated
1 Takumi runs a finance company.	☐	☐	☐
2 He spent ten hours a day at the computer or on his phone.	☐	☐	☐
3 He was stressed out because his business wasn't very successful.	☐	☐	☐
4 He was dissatisfied with his life.	☐	☐	☐
5 Takumi's doctor advised him to change his life.	☐	☐	☐
6 He decided to create an escape room in his apartment.	☐	☐	☐
7 The escape room has no machines in it.	☐	☐	☐
8 The sofas in the escape room are very comfortable.	☐	☐	☐
9 Takumi doesn't allow anyone into his escape room.	☐	☐	☐
10 His friends and co-workers thought his idea was weird.	☐	☐	☐

C Talking about ... managing stress

Step 1: Rank these situations from 1 (most stressful) to 8 (least stressful).

☐ taking exams   ☐ having too much to do

☐ giving a presentation   ☐ meeting new people

☐ looking for a parking space   ☐ telephoning in English

☐ traveling during rush hour   ☐ flying

Step 2: Work with a partner. Talk about your ranking and give reasons.

For me . . . is the most / the least stressful situation because . . .

Step 3: With your partner, make a list of what you can do to manage stress.

I do sports / go to the gym . . .   My girlfriend watches movies / does yoga . . .

Step 4: Work with another pair. Take turns to ask and answer questions about the things on your list from Step 3.

. . . helps me to relax. Have you ever tried it?
How did it feel? Was it effective for you? Why not?
Do you wish you could try . . . ? Why or why not?

▷ ▪ work-life balance ▪ time-out
▪ creative

I can understand an interview about escaping from the digital world.

4 Vocabulary focus
Time and money

A Which verbs can you use with *time* and *money*. Write *T* for time, *M* for money, and *B* for both.

☐ deposit   ☐ have   ☐ lend   ☐ run out of   ☐ tell (the)
☐ earn   ☐ invest ☐ lose   ☐ save   ☐ waste
☐ find   ☐ kill   ☐ make   ☐ spend

B Underline the correct word or phrase to complete the sentences.

> The meeting started at 9:00 AM.
>
> *I arrived on time.* = *I arrived at 9:00 AM.* (punctual, neither early nor late)
>
> *I arrived in time.* = *I arrived before 9:00 AM.* (with time to spare)

1 You waste money when you spend it on **useful / useless** things.
2 When you kill time, you do **important / unimportant** things to pass the time.
3 It is better not to **lend / borrow** money from anyone.
4 The 12:30 train arrived **in / on** time.
5 If you run out of time you have **a little / no** time left.
6 My employer **deposits / saves** my salary in my bank account.
7 You need to **save / invest** a lot of time to learn a foreign language.
8 I nearly forgot the appointment, but I remembered it just **in / on** time.

C Which is the odd word out?

1 arrange	☐ a meeting	☐ an appointment	☒ a deadline
2 keep	☐ up-to-date	☐ a plan	☐ track
3 meet	☐ an arrangement	☐ a deadline	☐ a client
4 miss	☐ a deadline	☐ a schedule	☐ an appointment
5 finish	☐ on schedule	☐ on time	☐ up-to-date
6 set	☐ priorities	☐ an agenda	☐ a time limit
7 manage	☐ stress	☐ work-life balance	☐ time

D Work with a partner. Take turns to ask and answer the questions.

1 Do you ever waste time or money? On what?
2 What is more important for you to have – time or money?
3 What would you do if you needed some money quickly?
4 What deadlines do you have to meet in everyday life?
5 What is a good work-life balance for you?

E Match the comments 1 to 5 with the responses A to E.

☐ **1** I don't like the way he wastes money.

☐ **2** I wish I knew how to make money quickly.

☐ **3** I'm a little low on money. Can you lend me some?

☐ **4** Have you ever invested any money?

☐ **5** Did you have enough money for your trip?

A Yes, but unfortunately I didn't make much profit.

B No, I ran out and had to borrow some.

C I know. He buys the most useless things.

D Sorry, I can't help you out. I don't have much either.

E You could go on a quiz show and win some.

F Work in groups of three. You have ten minutes to think of ways of saving money. The group with the most ideas wins!

- *switch off machines to save energy*
- *don't eat in restaurants*
- *. . .*

G ▷ **Key words** Look at the words at the bottom of pages 1–4. Choose the best words to complete the sentences.

1 Scott has to put in extra time because he is ....
2 If you feel you have a high .... you are satisfied with the way you live.
3 An electronic agenda can help you to .... of your appointments.
4 Takumi takes a .... in a special room.
5 Fortunately we are .... and will be able to meet the ....
6 You should set .... and do the important things first.
7 Tim is good at .... and organizes his work well.
8 Relaxing helps Takumi to be more ....

I can talk about time and money, using words that go together.

Reading
The wedding planners

A **Before you read** Work with a partner. Make a list of the things you need to organize for a wedding (e.g., clothes, a photographer, a venue for the ceremony, etc.). Then skim the article to see if you can find any of the things on your list.

Asian Business **Online**
looks at a booming business in South Korea.

Wedding planning is a US$15 billion industry in South Korea, thanks not only to Korean couples who use companies such as Your Wedding and Design-a-Wedding to organize their big day, but also to Chinese clients who love all things South Korean.

More than a quarter of all tourists to South Korea come from China, but the attraction for a small but growing number of wealthy couples is not the country's historic places and good food. They fly to Seoul or Jeju Island for the weekend to have wedding pictures taken!

Last year 2.5 million Chinese visitors paid between $2,000 and $4,000 for a wedding planner's package that includes transportation, hotel, interpreter, hairdressing, makeup, and a photograph album of wedding pictures.

The trend among the Chinese to copy the hairstyles, makeup, and fashions of South Korean celebrities has helped to boost the industry. "We always watch South Korean TV shows," says Zhang Li Jing from Beijing. "The singers and actors are just so stylish. We want to look our best in our wedding pictures, so we came here to Seoul."

After three hours with hairdressers and makeup artists, Li Jing and her bridegroom Feng are now ready for the photographer. They will spend the next six hours in front of the camera, with South Korean pop music in the background. Now and then helpers will refresh their makeup and attend to their hair.

Lim Seo-yun, deputy director of Design-a-Wedding says Chinese customers coming to Seoul total around 40 to 50 couples per month, and those going to Jeju Island about 20 to 30 couples per month on average. "These photo shoots are big business for South Korea," she says.

B **The main idea** Find and correct four mistakes in the text below.

Tourism is a US$15 billion industry in South Korea. Most tourists come from China. Li Jing and her bridegroom Feng have come to Jeju Island for a photo shoot. They love all things South Korean, especially the historic places and the food.

C **Comprehension** Complete the sentences

1 Korean couples use wedding planning companies to ....
2 Wealthy couples from China go to South Korea to ....
3 A wedding planner's package costs ....
4 A wedding planner's package includes ....
5 There is a trend in China to ....
6 Li Jing and Feng want to look as stylish as ....
7 During the photo shoot, Li Jing and Feng can listen to ....
8 Lim Seo-yun works as the ....

D **Now you** Are there any celebrities in your country that you admire? Why do you admire them?

I can understand an article about wedding planners in South Korea.

6 Culture focus
Who works the hardest?

A 🔊 Journalist Linda Reed is talking to Professor Stephen Leaver from the University of South Australia's Centre for Work+Life about his research into work hours in different countries. Listen to the conversation. Mark (✗) the countries you <u>don't</u> hear.

- ☐ Argentina
- ☐ Australia
- ☐ Austria
- ☐ Chile
- ☐ China
- ☐ Germany
- ☐ Hungary
- ☐ Indonesia
- ☐ Japan
- ☐ Poland
- ☐ Portugal
- ☐ South Korea

B 🔊 Listen to the conversation again and complete the sentences with a country from 6A.

1 About 40 percent of workers in .... think they work too hard.
2 .... and .... have a reputation for hard work.
3 The average work time in .... is now the same as in ....
4 The average number of work hours in some South American countries, for example .... and ...., is over 40 per week.
5 It's the same in some Eastern European countries, such as .... and ....
6 .... has a very high level of productivity.
7 .... and .... offer the most days off.
8 In .... the legal minimum is 10 days paid leave and in .... it is 15.

C 🔊 Listen again and answer the questions.

1 How many hours a week on average do the people work in . . .
   A Australia? ....
   B Japan? ....
   C South Korea? ....
   D Chile? ....
   E Poland? ....
   F Germany? ....
2 How much paid annual leave do workers have a right to in
   A Portugal and Austria? ....
   B Australia? ....
   C Japan? ....
   D South Korea? ....
3 How and why are work hours changing in Japan?
4 "Working longer doesn't mean working better." Give an example.
5 Why don't people in some countries take all the leave they are allowed?

How do I do it? I just stay the night.

D What do you know about work hours and annual leave in your country?

I can understand an interview about work hours in different countries.

Service industries

1 Business situation
Service providers

A) (4) Listen to four people talking about the services they provide. Match the speakers 1 to 4 with the pictures A to D.

Speaker 1 .... Speaker 2 .... Speaker 3 .... Speaker 4 ....

B) (4) Listen again and decide which statement 1 to 8 belongs to which service A to D.

A party service	C translation service
B lunch delivery service	D personal assistant service

1 We can organize theater tickets for you at any time.   D
2 You can trust us with your personal documents. ....
3 Call us if you want a healthy meal. ....
4 We will do your errands quickly and correctly. ....
5 We are the best in the business, and we guarantee a high standard. ....
6 We have a reputation for quality and speed. ....
7 All our food is prepared at home. ....
8 I can organize anything from a cleaner to a party. ....

C) **Now you** Which other service providers do you know about? Which services do you use?

▷ ▪ to provide ▪ errands ▪ recommendation
▪ reputation ▪ reliable

I can understand people talking about the services they provide.

Focus 1: Causative *get something done* and *have something done*

A 🔊 **4** Listen to the speakers in 1A again. Who said what? Write *T* for Timothy, *E* for Emily, *S* for Sayaka, and *V* for Vincent.

1 A lot of foreign companies **get** their product brochures **translated** into Japanese. ....
2 If someone wants to **have** their apartment **cleaned**, I can organize a cleaner. ....
3 They **have** home-cooked food **delivered** to their offices. ....
4 Busy people **get** their parties **organized** by party services like mine. ....
5 Many of my clients want to **have** personal documents **translated** into English. ....
6 I **get** them **done** by freelance translators. ....
7 I **get** the drinks **delivered**. ....
8 If they want to **have** errands **done**, I can do them. ....
9 I **have** the food **prepared** in a good restaurant. ....

B Look at the sentences in 2A and complete the rule.

When we say that we don't do something ourselves but ask or pay someone else to do it, we use the verbs .... or .... + object + past participle.

Get or *have something done* can be used in all tenses:

I'm having my documents translated.   *I've had a pizza delivered twice this week.*

Yesterday I got my car washed.   *Tomorrow I will have the letter sent.*

C Put the words in the correct order.

1 printed / to get / some business cards / going / are you ?
2 do / delivered / have / you / your lunch / usually ?
3 you / to get / manage / your computer / repaired / did ?
4 the company / built / new headquarters / is having
5 taken / get / have to / I / a passport photograph

D Work with a partner.

Student A: Go to Partner file 1.
Student B: Ask your partner questions about the things you can see in your pictures. Answer his/her questions about their pictures. Ask three questions for each picture. Use *have* or *get something done*.

1 *Have you ever gotten / had ...?*   2 *How often do you ...?*   3 *When did you last ...?*

A cut – hair   B dry-clean – clothes   C translate – document   D repair – phone screen

▷ ▪ freelance ▪ to set standards
   ▪ to set up a business

I can use the forms get/have something done.

Grammar focus
Focus 2: Quantifiers

E 🔊 **4** Listen to the speakers in 1A again. Complete the sentences and then complete the chart.

Speaker 1: In our busy society .... and .... people don't have enough time to do all the things they have to do.

Speaker 2: Our business is booming and there are .... problems than we expected. .... new customers come on recommendation.

Speaker 3: I don't make a lot of money because I prefer to do .... translations and do them well.

Speaker 4: Busy people who like to give parties, but have .... time.
I had a .... difficulties setting up the business, but now I have regular customers.
I earn .... money now, but I enjoy my job much more.

	Comparative	Superlative
much, many	....	most
(a) little	....	least
(a)	....	fewest

F Underline the correct word to complete the rule.

> *(A) little, less,* and *least* are used with **singular / plural** nouns.
> *(A) few, fewer,* and *fewest* are used with **singular / plural** nouns.

G Complete the sentences with words from the chart in 2E.

	Lisa	Tony	Amy
Business	baby-sitting service	cleaning service	pizza delivery service
Customers	3	12	30
Workdays	4 per week	5 per week	7 per week
Work hours	5 per day	8 per day	6 per day
Revenue	$800 per month	$1,000 per month	$1,200 per month

1 Lisa only has a .... customers, Tony has .... customers than Lisa, but Amy has the ....

2 Amy works seven days a week. Tony works .... days than Amy, but Lisa works the ....

3 Tony earns .... than Amy, but Lisa earns the ....

4 Amy works .... hours a day than Lisa, but .... hours than Tony.

> *I can* use little, less, least and few, fewer, fewest.

A ▶5 Nora Susanti works in the Customer Service Department of the Coffee Bean Company in Indonesia. The company sells franchises to people who want to open a Coffee Bean shop. Listen to her conversation and number the steps in the correct order from 1 to 5.

A The caller fills out some forms and sends them back. ....
B Nora takes down some information about the caller. 1
C Nora has some forms sent to the caller by email. ....
D A company representative contacts the caller. ....
E Nora sends a test mail. ....

B ▶5 Listen to the conversation again and answer the questions.

1 What is the main purpose of the call?
2 How long does it take for a rep to make contact?
3 What information does Nora ask the caller to give her?
4 How will the caller get some information in advance?
5 What does the company want to know about people who apply for a franchise?

C **Talking about ...** successful franchise companies

Student A: Go to Partner file 2.
Student B: Ask Student A questions about Subway and fill in the missing information.

Subway

If you're hungry, it's the easiest thing to *(do what?)* .... At any Subway restaurant, you can *(do what?)* .... The person who makes your sandwich is called a *(what?)* "..........." Your sandwich will be made with *(what?)* .... The company was founded in the United States in *(when?)* .... Now, Subway has more than *(how many?)* .... global locations. All new franchise owners have to *(do what?)* .... The time is spent *(where?)* .... They take an exam *(when?)* .... If they pass the exam, they can *(do what)* ....

Now answer Student A's questions with information from the text below.

United Parcel Service

With the help of UPS, you can have a parcel sent quickly to almost anywhere at any time. The company was founded at the beginning of the twentieth century. It was a time when more and more businesses and private individuals needed to get errands done and messages delivered. UPS founder, James Casey, saw a business opportunity, so he borrowed $100 to set up his own business. Most deliveries were made on foot or by bicycle. Today UPS delivers 16 million packages and documents a day by airplane, ship, and truck. One important condition for new UPS franchise owners is that they have to be good in English and have to pass an exam to prove it.

▷ ▪ to apply ▪ franchise ▪ representative (rep)

I can understand a call center conversation and talk about franchise companies.

4 Vocabulary focus
Focus 1: Jobs in the service industry

A Match the service providers 1 to 8 with the services A to H.

1 A tourist agent	A helps companies to find staff.
2 A logistics company	B provides telephone and Internet services.
3 An accountant	C organizes conferences.
4 A catering service	D organizes transportation of goods.
5 A technical support service	E controls a company's finances.
6 A recruitment service	F provides food and drinks.
7 A telecom company	G arranges vacations and trips.
8 An event manager	H solves technical problems.

B Use one of the verbs in the correct form and one of the service providers in 1A, 2G, or 4A to complete the sentences. There is one extra verb.

~~arrange~~	assist	clean	deliver	do
look after	organize	provide	translate	

1 To have a vacation ...., call a(n) ....
   To have a vacation arranged, call a travel agent.
2 To have your children ....,
   call a(n) ....
3 To have a text ...., call a(n) ....
4 To get food and drink ....,
   call a(n) ....
5 To have your apartment ....,
   call a(n) ....
6 To get some errands ....,
   call a(n) ....
7 To have some parcels ....,
   call a(n) ....
8 To get a conference ...., call a(n) ....

> An *employer* gives work to his or her *employees*.
> A *trainer* trains *trainees* on the job.
> A *franchiser* gives franchise licenses to *franchisees*.

C Complete the chart with words from 1A, 3A, and 3C.

Adjective	Noun		Verb	Noun
....	flexibility		to assist	....
....	convenience		....	delivery
....	creation		to found	....
difficult	....		to franchise	....
....	help		to recommend	....
....	reliability		to represent	....

D Choose one of the service providers mentioned in this unit. Don't tell your partner. Your partner has to ask questions to find out what the service is.

Does the person . . . ?

> *I can* talk about different jobs in the service industry.

4 Vocabulary focus
Focus 2: Giving and receiving information

E 🔊 6 Listen to a conversation between Sayaka Okazaki and a caller who wants to have a document translated. Mark (✗) the two phrases that are NOT in the conversation.

- ☐ Could you tell me something about . . .
- ☐ I'm afraid I can't say until . . .
- ☐ Let me see if I've got this right.
- ☐ Thanks for the information.
- ☐ I need some information about . . .
- ☐ I have another question.
- ☐ I'd rather not say.
- ☐ That depends on . . .

> *I'd rather* wait for the document = I would prefer to . . .
> *I'd rather not* read the report now. = I would prefer not to . . .

F Which phrase in 4E . . .

1 asks for information? ....
2 gives information? ....
3 avoids giving information? ....
4 asks for further information? ....
5 checks information? ....

G Work with a partner. Read the transcript for the conversation in 4E on page 98. Write a similar conversation between a caller and a different service provider (see 1A or 4A for ideas). Use phrases from 4E. Ask for, give, and check information about:

costs
time
contact details

Decide on your roles and play your conversation to the class.

H ▷ **Key words** Look at the words at the bottom of pages 9–12. Choose the best words to complete the sentences.

1 Where can we .... for a .... ?
2 Do you have a .... for a .... party service?
3 Vincent has .... very high .... for his business.
4 I need a personal assistant to do my ....
5 A catering service .... the food and drink for our last conference.
6 Sayaka gets .... translators to translate French and German.
7 You need a good business head to ....
....
8 Timothy has a good .... for first-class service.

I can give, receive, and check information.

A **Before you read** What kind of things does a courier service deliver?

Asian Business **Online**
looks at Japanese delivery services.

Very few countries enjoy delivery services as good as the *takkyubin* services in Japan. They are so common there that the Japanese can't imagine life without them. Parcels, luggage, sports equipment, frozen food, and furniture – whatever you can think of, you can have it picked up from and delivered to any address in the country, including private homes, offices, hotels, and airports. Yamato Transport started the first service in the 1970s, and although there are now several other delivery service companies, Yamato's *Takkyubin* service remains the market leader. *Takkyubin* is actually a brand name, but it has also come to be the word used for courier services in general.

With *takkyubin* you are extremely flexible. Going on a ski vacation? No need to carry your skis; just have them sent to your destination. Going on a business trip? You can have your suitcases picked up from your home and sent to your hotel. If you're away on a long trip, you can get a suitcase with fresh clothes picked up and brought to your hotel, and souvenir shops will send a package with your holiday gifts directly to your family and friends.

The services are wonderfully convenient. You can arrange for a pick-up time that suits you, and if you are not home for a delivery, you can pick it up from your local convenience store. Delivery is usually the next day and prices are reasonable. You can have a suitcase picked up from an address in Tokyo and taken to an address in Osaka for about 2,000 yen, which is less than US$20, including insurance. The 1,600-kilometer trip from Tokyo to Okinawa takes two days and costs about 3,000 yen – a small investment for excellent service. No wonder other countries wish they were as lucky as the Japanese!

B **Scanning for detail** Find examples of using a delivery service for:

1 luggage   2 sports equipment   3 packages

C **Comprehension** Are the statements correct? If not, correct them.

1 The *takkyubin* service will deliver to any country in the world.
2 The word *takkyubin* refers only to Yamato Transport's delivery service.
3 It isn't important if you are not at home when a delivery is made.
4 Delivery normally takes two days.
5 Deliveries over long distances are not expensive.

D **Vocabulary in context**

Find nouns in the article from the verbs.
1 invest   2 lead   3 insure   4 deliver   5 furnish   6 ski

E Match the words from the article.

1 reasonable	E	5 sports	....	A homes	E ~~prices~~
2 wonderfully	....	6 private	....	B service	F equipment
3 convenience	....	7 brand	....	C clothes	G store
4 fresh	....	8 courier	....	D convenient	H name

F **Now you** Have you used a delivery service? What did you use it for?

I can understand an article about Japanese delivery services.

Business writing
Placing an order

A **[7]** **Listen to Nancy Green ordering work clothes for her cleaning company's workers. Check (✔) the items they talk about.**

- ☐ aprons
- ☐ blouses
- ☐ caps
- ☐ jeans
- ☐ rubber gloves
- ☐ T-shirts

B **Listen again and fill in the purchase order.**

From: nancygreen@cleanmachine.com
To: benjohnson@bj-workwear.com
Subject: Purchase order

Dear Ben:

As per our phone call, we would like to place the following order:

Quantity	Item	Color	Size	Price per item
....	apron	....	M	$10
....	apron	....	L	$10
5	....	white	S	....
5	....	white	M	....
....	T-shirt	white	....	$15
....	T-shirt	white	....	$15
25	pair rubber gloves	....	M	....
25	pair rubber gloves	....	L	....

Please confirm the five percent discount on the total price as discussed and that we can expect delivery within three days. Payment is due within ten days of receipt of delivery as usual.

C **Find words in the purchase order in 6B that mean:**

1 arrival of letters, goods, or packages ....
2 noun from "receive" ....
3 amount of money taken off the price ....
4 a formal word for "thing" ....
5 make an agreement official ....
6 another word for "buy" ....

D **Find the phrase in the purchase order in 6B that Nancy uses to . . .**

1 say the company wants to order something. ....
2 make sure the discount is not forgotten. ....
3 say when the company will receive the goods. ....
4 confirm when they have to pay for the goods. ....

E **[8]** **Vincent Chen calls the California Wine Shop to order some drinks. Listen to the conversation. Write Vincent's purchase order. Use the purchase order in 6B to help you. Prices are in New Taiwan dollars (NT$).**

Subject: Purchase order

Dear Mike,

I would like . . .

Quantity	Item	Price per item
12 bottles (1.5 liters)	mineral water	20 NT$

I can understand and write a purchase order.

TOEIC® practice

1 Listening

A) 🔊9 Photographs Listen. Then choose the sentence that best describes the photograph.

1 A ☐   B ☐   C ☐   D ☐   2 A ☐   B ☐   C ☐   D ☐

B) 🔊10 Question-Response Listen carefully. Choose the best response to the sentence you hear.

Example: Which time is better for you – morning or afternoon?

         A ☑ I'm free after lunch.

         B ☐ Sorry, I've no idea what the time is.

         C ☐ OK, I'll be there on time.

1 A ☐   B ☐   C ☐   3 A ☐   B ☐   C ☐

2 A ☐   B ☐   C ☐   4 A ☐   B ☐   C ☐

2 Speaking

A) Describe a picture Choose one of the pictures in 1A. Look at it for 30 seconds, then describe it in your own words.

B) 🔊11 Respond to questions In this part of the test, you will answer THREE questions. For each question you must answer immediately after the beep. You have 15 seconds to respond to questions 1 and 2 and 30 seconds to respond to question 3.

Imagine an international marketing company is doing research in your country. You have agreed to take part in a television interview about your leisure time.

Question 1
How much leisure time do you have each week?

Question 2
What kinds of things do you like to do in your leisure time?

Question 3
Describe your favorite leisure time activity.

3 Reading

Incomplete sentences Choose the best word to complete each sentence.

1 I wish I .... more leisure time.

- ☐ **A** did have
- ☐ **B** have
- ☐ **C** will have
- ☐ **D** had

2 Amy works .... hours per day than Tony.

- ☐ **A** less
- ☐ **B** fewer
- ☐ **C** many
- ☐ **D** few

3 It's important to finish .... schedule.

- ☐ **A** on
- ☐ **B** in
- ☐ **C** by
- ☐ **D** at

4 You have to .... priorities.

- ☐ **A** keep
- ☐ **B** do
- ☐ **C** set
- ☐ **D** manage

5 A(n) .... service helps companies to find staff.

- ☐ **A** employee
- ☐ **B** recruitment
- ☐ **C** catering
- ☐ **D** logistics

6 It's a good idea .... a foreign language.

- ☐ **A** learn
- ☐ **B** learning
- ☐ **C** learns
- ☐ **D** to learn

4 Writing

Write a sentence based on a picture Write ONE sentence based on each picture. You must use the two words or phrases that are given with the picture.

Example: have / remove
Possible answer: *We must have the tree removed.*

1 get / car wash

2 meeting / fewer than

Marketing

1 Business situation
The four Ps

A 〖12〗 **Eric and Andy are taking part in an online training course in marketing. Listen to today's webinar and match the four Ps (1–4) with their definitions (A–D).**

1 Product	A the cost of goods and services
2 Price	B persuading people to buy goods and services
3 Promotion	C goods or services for sale
4 Place	D where goods and services are sold

B 〖12〗 **At the end of his talk, the marketing expert asked the students for questions. Read Eric and Andy's questions. Listen again and find the answers.**

1 **Eric:** Could you repeat what you said at the beginning about the fourth *P*?
2 **Andy:** Please could you explain again why the image of a product is just as important as the product itself?
3 **Eric:** Have I got this right: Customers won't buy a product if it is very expensive?
4 **Andy:** You said something about a logo. What was it again, please?
5 **Eric:** You mentioned four ways of advertising. Could you repeat them, please?
6 **Andy:** Did you say that there's no point in having expensive promotion campaigns?

C 〖13〗 **Listen to four people talking about different products. Which of the four Ps are they referring to?**

Speaker 1 ....   Speaker 2 ....   Speaker 3 ....   Speaker 4 ....

D **You work for the tourist board in your country. The board wants to market your city or region to attract more tourists. Work in small groups. Decide together:**

• Who is your main target group (age – nationality)?
• What makes your product (your city/region) special?
• What positive things will you stress?
• Is there a negative image you should correct (dangerous – overcrowded – bad climate)?
• How and where will you advertise your product?

▷ ▪ promotion ▪ value for the money
    ▪ market research ▪ trendy

I can understand some basic marketing ideas.

Grammar focus
Focus 1: Review of gerunds

A Look at this extract from the webinar. Underline examples of gerunds.

1 As the subject of a sentence, e.g., **Finding** the right target group is very important.
2 After a verb, e.g., We should consider **lowering** the price.
3 After a preposition, e.g., What are the advantages of **advertising** on the Internet?

Marketing is all about putting the right product at the right price in the right place at the right time. This mix is known as the "the four Ps." The first two Ps stand for product and price – that means providing customers with a product at a price they feel is fair. Informing customers about the product and persuading them to buy it is known as promotion. The fourth P stands for place, which is about making the product easily available.

B Read the rest of the transcript for the webinar in 1A on page 100 and find more examples of gerunds 1, 2, and 3 in 2A.

Stop doing something = give up doing something:
I stopped buying expensive clothes years ago.

Stop to do something = stop in order to do something else:
I was driving home and I stopped to have coffee.

C Use the verbs in the gerund form to complete the sentences.

advertise   buy   carry   identify   interrupt
lose   promote   shop   start   think

1 .... on the Internet is known as webvertising.
2 Do you enjoy .... for clothes?
3 Are you interested in .... the latest smartphone?
4 Have you tried .... your products at a trade show?
5 .... someone when they are speaking is impolite.
6 We succeeded in .... our target group.
7 .... a new sales campaign is a bit risky right now.
8 We don't want to risk .... any customers.
9 .... out market research is extremely important.
10 She's really good at .... up new marketing strategies.

87% of the 56% who completed more than 23% of the survey thought it was a waste of time

D **Now you** Complete the statements about yourself. Use the gerund form of the verb. Compare your statements with a partner.

1 I'm interested in ....
2 .... is very important to me.
3 I'm looking forward to ....
4 I can't imagine ....
5 .... is quite difficult for me.
6 I'm worried about ....
7 I enjoy ....
8 I always get excited about ....

▷ ▪ to compete ▪ to promote
   ▪ target group

I can use the gerund as subject or object and after prepositions.

2 Grammar focus

Focus 2: Definite and indefinite articles

E Look at the sentences and complete the rule with *a*, *an*, *the*, or *no article*.

That's why the image of **a product** is just as important as **the product** itself.
The product has to look special so that **people** will want to have it.
Your product must be easily available to **the people** who want to buy it.

> 1 We use the indefinite article .... (or ....) when we refer to a person or thing for the first time, or when we mean "any one, not a particular one."
> 2 We use the definite article .... when we name something for a second time, or when it is clear which person or thing we are talking about.
> 3 When we talk about people or things in general, we use ....

F Complete the sentences with *a*, *an*, *the*, or *no article*. Then compare with a partner.

> Remember we use *the* with superlative adjectives:
>
> *He's the richest man in the world.*

1 I don't usually mind .... exams, but .... exams we took last week were really hard.
2 .... English is a world language.
3 .... English I learned at school was American English.
4 **A:** I'm going to .... local store. Can I get you anything?
   B: Yes, would you bring me .... newspaper, please?
5 I don't go to .... meetings very often.
6 .... meetings we have in our company are long and boring.
7 I own .... red bicycle and .... orange one .... red one is new, but I've had .... orange one for a long time.
8 **A:** Is there .... bank nearby?
   B: I'm afraid .... nearest one is about a mile away.

Do you speak English?

G Work with a partner. There are 12 mistakes with the articles in the text. Correct the mistakes.

> We use *the* when there is only one:
>
> *the sun*, *the moon*, *the world*, *the Pacific Ocean*

market research

Before you launch ~~the~~ *a* new product onto the market, it is important to do a market research to find out more about group you want to target. That means gathering the information about people's needs and preferences. You can do this by carrying out the door-to-door survey, or getting people to fill out the questionnaires or take part in the telephone interview. Telephone interviews are most inexpensive method, and speed of such surveys is another advantage. You can quickly make contact with potential customers all over a world. A data you gather will help you decide where to place your product and ways of advertising that you should choose.

....

▷ ▪ to launch ▪ data

I can use definite and indefinite articles.

A) |14| Three young people are talking about the reasons they buy certain products. Listen to the conversation and check (✔) the reasons each person gives.

Reason	Dave	Misaki	Miguel
1 wants to look cool			
2 wants the cheapest product			
3 thinks the brand is a good value for the money			
4 likes the brand image			
5 wants to impress people			
6 The product has special features he/she wants.			
7 prefers no-name products			
8 can rely on the quality of a brand name			
9 likes to have the same things as his/her friends			

B) Work with a partner. Give reasons why would you buy:

| a cell phone | clothes | drinks | a shampoo | sports shoes | a tablet |

C) Talking about ... brands and logos

Work with a partner. Look at these famous logos and answer the questions. Then compare your answers with another pair.

1 Which products are these logos connected with?
2 What is the image of the products? (*traditional, trendy, luxury, mass market, . . . ?*)
3 Who is the target group? (*age – income – male/female?*)
4 Can you name some well-known competitors for these products?
5 Have you ever bought any products with these logos? Were you satisfied with them?
6 Do you own any products with other famous brand names? Which ones? Why did you buy them?
7 How important are brand names to you personally? (*I always / don't often / never look for brand names when I buy . . . because . . .*)
8 Describe one of your favorite products. Does it make your life better or easier?

▷ ▪ to brainwash ▪ competitor

I can understand a conversation and talk about brands and logos.

Vocabulary focus

Focus 1: Marketing vocabulary

A Put the missing words into the puzzle. The words are all in this unit.

Across

1 Pepsi and Rolex are famous . . .
4 An advertising . . . can be very expensive.
6 Advertising in the street
9 The opposite of "trendy"
10 When you carry out a . . . you ask a lot of people questions.

Down

2 If you can't find a product anywhere, it's not . . .
3 A picture or symbol of a company
5 Advertising on the Internet
7 A person who buys and uses products or services
8 The material used to pack products

B Match the verbs 1 to 8 with the nouns A to H. Use each word only once.

1 convince ....
2 design ....
3 fix ....
4 gather ....
5 launch ....
6 plan ....
7 satisfy ....
8 analyze ....

A a campaign
B behavior
C a logo
D a need
E a product
F data
G a price
H a customer

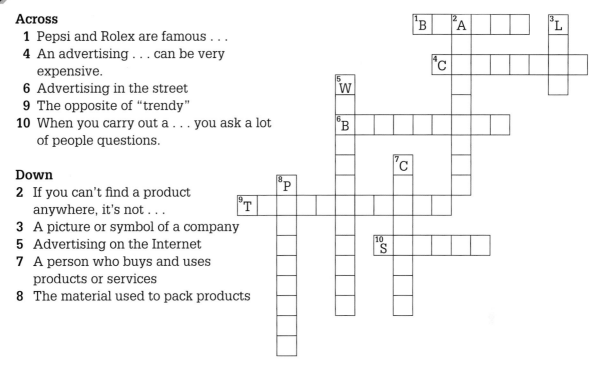

C Complete the sentences with the correct preposition.

across	at	for	in (2x)	on (2x)	out (3x)	up

1 There's no point *in* spending money *on* TV commercials.
2 You have to offer the product .... a fair price.
3 We are going to put our product .... the market in spring.
4 Dave thinks his sneakers are a good value .... the money.
5 We have decided to carry .... a door-to-door survey.
6 Hundreds of people took part .... the survey.
7 They were asked to fill .... a questionnaire.
8 What's the best way to get our message .... ?
9 She likes to keep .... with the latest fashion.
10 The salesperson pointed .... the advantages.

I can use a lot of different marketing words.

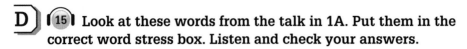

4 Vocabulary focus
Focus 2: Word stress

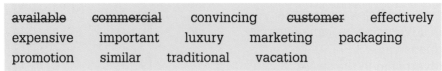

D **15** Look at these words from the talk in 1A. Put them in the correct word stress box. Listen and check your answers.

~~available~~   ~~commercial~~   convincing   ~~customer~~   effectively
expensive   important   luxury   marketing   packaging
promotion   similar   traditional   vacation

●••	•●•	•●••
customer	*commercial*	*available*

E Six of the ten words below can be nouns or verbs. Underline them.

announce   compete   decrease   discuss   export
increase   message   protest   record   research

F Use the underlined words in 4E in the correct form to complete the sentences (1–5). Underline the stressed syllable and then read your sentences aloud to a partner.

> Some words have a different stress as a noun or a verb:
> **Im**ports *have increased.* (= noun)
> *The country im***ports** *a lot of goods.* (= verb)

1 Market .... is important for the success of a product. Our product was not a success because we .... (not) our target group correctly.
2 We are pleased to announce that sales have .... The .... is a result of good advertising.
3 Our region .... a lot of high-tech products to other countries. Unfortunately, ... to the United States .... last month. The .... was due to economic problems.
4 This is the hottest summer on .... Scientists have .... temperatures for more than a hundred years.
5 Last year, customers .... against the rise in prices. Because of the .... , the company lowered its prices again.

G ▷ **Key words** Look at the words at the bottom of pages 19–22. Choose the best words to complete the sentences.

1 .... aims to persuade people to buy goods or services.
2 Lee likes to be .... and follows the latest fashions.
3 We did a lot of .... to find out what our .... wanted.
4 When you .... a new product, you put it onto the market for the first time.
5 We have better products than our ....
6 You can only .... effectively if the four *P*s mix is right.
7 Some people think that advertising is a kind of ....
8 The .... from the market survey was used to .... the new product.

> *I can* stress the correct syllable in different words.

Reading
Lucky or unlucky?

A) Before you read What numbers or colors do people in your country think are lucky or unlucky.

Asian Business **Online**
looks at lucky numbers and colors in product promotion.

Have you ever wondered why the Beijing Olympics began officially on August 8, 2008 (8/8/08)? Or why skyscrapers in New York have no floor number 13? The answer is that in many Asian countries eight is a lucky number, and in much of the Western world thirteen is an unlucky number, while seven is generally considered lucky.

If a company wants to promote its products abroad, it is important to know the lucky and unlucky numbers in the target country. The number four is unlucky in China, Korea, and Japan because it sounds like the word for "death," so it isn't a good idea to have the number four in a brand name. Alfa Romeo changed the name of a new model 144 car in Singapore because people were afraid to buy it.

Positive or negative associations with numbers can also influence pricing. In the West, prices often end in nine (e.g., $399). In many Asian countries, nine is unlucky, so prices in China, Japan, and Korea often end in eight. It might be wise for Western companies to adjust their prices to include lucky numbers – the more the better!

Colors can also be associated with good luck or bad luck, and this should be considered when designing logos, advertising, and packaging. Red is generally considered to bring good luck and happiness in both East and West, while black is the color of death. White is also associated with death and funerals in some Asian countries and should not be used for product packaging.

Blue is probably the safest global color because it is associated with wealth. But even then it's not that simple. When a well-known beverage company changed its vending machines from dark blue to light blue in Southeast Asia, sales fell. Light blue is associated with death in that region.

B) Skim the text and find out which numbers and colors are lucky or unlucky in:

1 Asian countries.   2 Western countries.

C) Meaning in context Find these words in the text. Can you guess their meaning? How did you guess?

abroad   to adjust   funeral   associated   vending machine

D) Scanning for detail Complete the sentences with information from the article.

1 Skyscrapers in New York have no thirteenth floor because ....
2 Four is considered unlucky in some Asian countries because ....
3 People in Singapore didn't want to buy Alfa Romeo model 144 because ....
4 A price of $888 would be good for a product in Korea because ....
5 Colors are important when companies design ....
6 In most parts of the world blue is associated with ....
7 A vending machine company's sales fell in Southeast Asia when .... because ....

I can understand an article about lucky and unlucky numbers and colors.

Culture focus
Gift-giving customs and etiquette

A 〔16〕 **Rob Hall from the company Asia-Pacific Business Specialists is talking about gift-giving customs in the business world. Listen and decide if the statements are true or false. Correct the false statements.**

1 Businesspeople don't usually give gifts in North America and the UK.
2 It is usual to give gifts to government employees in Singapore.
3 Gifts in Japan should always be well wrapped.
4 You should never give expensive gifts in China.
5 It is not a good idea to give things in pairs in China.
6 It is not usual to exchange business gifts in Indonesia.
7 Gift giving in Thailand is very formal.
8 When you give a gift in Thailand, you should bow.

B 〔16〕 **Listen again and check (✔) the countries.**

1 Business gifts might be seen as a bribe in . . .
   ☐ the United States ☐ Malaysia ☐ Japan ☐ the UK
2 You should present and accept a gift with both hands in . . .
   ☐ China ☐ Indonesia ☐ Japan ☐ Thailand
3 It is OK to refuse a gift at least once in . . .
   ☐ China ☐ Indonesia ☐ Japan ☐ Thailand
4 Gifts are not opened in front of the giver in . . .
   ☐ the United States ☐ Indonesia ☐ China ☐ the UK

C 〔16〕 **Now listen for words that mean:**

1 unusual, hard to find
2 a gift given to influence a person
3 the opposite of "extravagant"
4 turn down, say "no"
5 discouraged, dissatisfied
6 not allow
7 a pleasing combination of things
8 understanding and enjoying something

You'll never guess what I got you...

Reynolds

D **Now you** Work with a partner and make lists. Compare your lists with another pair.

1 On what occasions do people exchange gifts in your country?
2 What should visitors to your country know about gift-giving customs and etiquette? Think about these things:

colors	correct ways to give and receive gifts	
numbers	suitable gifts	unsuitable gifts

I can understand and talk about gift-giving customs.

Problems and conflicts

1 Business situation
Problems at work

A [17] Amy Wang works for an international company in Taiwan. She is talking to her co-worker Kristin about some problems she is having at work. Listen to the conversation and choose the correct answer.

1 Amy's problem is that she doesn't
- ☐ **A** like her job anymore.
- ☐ **B** get along with her project manager.
- ☐ **C** know her co-workers very well.

2 When Ken Tsai came into the office yesterday, Amy was
- ☐ **A** expecting him.
- ☐ **B** working at her computer.
- ☐ **C** making a private phone call.

3 Kristin thinks Ken Tsai
- ☐ **A** isn't a very nice person.
- ☐ **B** was right to tell Amy off.
- ☐ **C** was wrong to tell Amy off.

4 Amy didn't finish the report because
- ☐ **A** it was lunchtime.
- ☐ **B** she needed some statistics.
- ☐ **C** there were some technical problems.

5 Amy kept making mistakes because
- ☐ **A** she felt nervous.
- ☐ **B** Ken was standing behind her.
- ☐ **C** she was incompetent.

6 Amy's solution to her problem is to
- ☐ **A** ask for a transfer.
- ☐ **B** talk to Ken Tsai.
- ☐ **C** move to Kristin's department.

B What problems might the people below have at work? Give reasons for your answers.

1 sales assistant   **2** taxi driver   **3** teacher   **4** receptionist

1 *Customers are not always polite. Perhaps the job is boring.*

▷ ▪ fault ▪ to blame
▪ incompetent ▪ working atmosphere

I can understand and talk about problems at work.

Grammar focus
Focus 1: Reported speech (1)

A **17** Listen to the conversation in 1A again. Complete the sentences in reported speech.

Direct speech	Reported speech
"I **love** my job."	You always said that ....
"You **are** wasting the company's time."	He said ....
"The report **isn't** finished."	I told him that ....

B Complete the rule.

> When we report statements, we change the present tense to the .... tense.

C Read what Amy said to the human resources manager. Later Amy reported the conversation to Kristin. What did she tell her?

"I'm so unhappy that I don't look forward to coming to work anymore. I can't get along with Ken Tsai. He always seems to find me out at the wrong moment, and he makes me feel incompetent. He sometimes comes into my office and stands behind me. He watches me while I'm working and I don't like it. He blames me for things that aren't my fault, and if things go wrong, he doesn't give me a chance to explain. I can't put up with it any longer, and I want to ask for a transfer to another department."

I told her that I was unhappy and . . . I said I . . . Then I told her he . . .

D Amy told Kristin what the human resources manager said to her. Read Amy's report and write down what the manager said in direct speech.

She said that Ken Tsai was really a very nice person. Perhaps he was a little bit unsure of himself because he was new in the company and he felt responsible for the success of the project. She said she wanted me to talk to him personally about my problems. She suggested a meeting with all three of us in her office. She said if that didn't work, I could still ask for a transfer to another department, but she thought it best to try an open discussion first.

What's the problem, Amy?

"Ken Tsai is really a very nice person. Perhaps . . ."

> Pronouns also change:
>
> "I love my job." → You said that you loved your job.

▷ ▪ human resources ▪ transfer

I can use reported speech in statements.

E Underline the verbs which are NOT in the simple past.

1 I was calling a friend on my cell phone when he came into the office.
2 I was working on some statistics when my computer crashed.
3 When I turned around, Ken was standing behind me.

F Complete the rule in sentence 1. Underline the correct tense in 2.

1 We form the past continuous with ..../*were* and the .... form of the verb.
2 We use the **past continuous** / **simple past** tense for completed actions in the past. We use the **past continuous** / **simple past** tense for actions in progress in the past.

G Two of Amy's co-workers had a bad day at work yesterday. Complete the sentences. Use the simple past and the past continuous.

Some verbs we don't use with the continuous form, for example:

be, like, know, prefer, understand, want.

Ben

I **1** .... (ride) my bike to work when I **2** .... (see) a pretty girl. While I **3** .... (try) to look cool, I **4** .... (fall) off my bike! It **5** .... (be) already late when I **6** .... (arrive) at our building, then the elevator **7** .... (get) stuck while I **8** .... (go) up to my office. When I **9** .... (open) the office door, my boss **10** .... (wait) for me. He **11** .... (not be) very pleased. At lunchtime, I **12** .... (have) a sandwich in the cafeteria when somebody **13** .... (spill) tea on me! In the afternoon, I **14** .... (want) to make some phone calls. I **15** .... (talk) to an important customer when I **16** .... (lose) the signal. It was a very frustrating day.

Lin

I **1** .... (travel) to work on the subway when I **2** .... (notice) that I didn't have my phone with me and I hate to be without it. When I **3** .... (get) to work, a co-worker **4** .... (sit) in my office. She **5** .... (ask) if she could use my computer because a technician **6** .... (work) on hers. While she **7** .... (use) my computer, she **8** .... (delete) all my files! I **9** .... (try) to call the hotline, and I **10** .... (wait) for them to answer the phone when I **11** .... (realize) that I was late for a meeting. On the way home I **12** .... (hurt) my foot while I **13** .... (run) to the subway. It really wasn't a good day.

H Work with a partner. Ask and answer three questions for these situations.

1 have an accident
   Have you ever *had an accident?*
   What were you doing when *you had the accident?*
   What did you do after *you had the accident?*
2 see an accident
3 cut your finger
4 lose your cell phone
5 hear a strange noise in the night
6 your computer crashes

I can use the past continuous.

Listening and speaking
Working as a "farang" boss

A | **18** | Listen to the interview with Stan Walker about working as a foreign or "farang" boss in Thailand. Check (✔) the dos and don'ts for foreign bosses.

		Do	Don't
1	Expect to make team-based decisions.	☐	☐
2	Think that "yes" means "yes."	☐	☐
3	Double-check that your instructions were understood.	☐	☐
4	Focus mainly on your targets.	☐	☐
5	Socialize with your employees.	☐	☐
6	Show your feelings when you are angry.	☐	☐
7	Solve conflicts openly.	☐	☐

B | **18** | Listen to the interview again and answer the questions.

1 Why did Stan decide to go to work in Thailand?
2 Why was it hard for him to be the boss of Thai employees?
3 Stan talks about two ways to have some fun with employees. What are they?
4 What does "lose face" mean?
5 What are Stan's tips for a happy and successful stay in Thailand?

C **Talking about ...** solving conflicts

Step 1: Put the phrases into one of the boxes. Compare your answers with a partner.

I hate to say this, but . . .
I find it unacceptable that . . .
Could you give me an example?
There's something I'd like to discuss with you.

I'm sorry. I have no excuse.
I'm sorry about that, but (+ excuse) . . .
It's embarrassing for me to say this.
That's simply not true!

Criticizing	Responding to criticism
I hate to say this, but . . .	I'm sorry. I have no excuse.

Step 2: Think about what you would do and say in these situations:

1 Your boss always criticizes your work and makes you feel incompetent.
2 Your co-worker is lazy and leaves most of the work for you.
3 It's midnight and your neighbor is playing loud music.
4 You are in line at the supermarket when someone cuts in front of you.
5 One of your co-workers often bullies a younger co-worker.

Step 3: Work with a partner. Tell each other your ideas for Step 2.

Step 4: With your partner, choose one of the situations in Step 2. Write a dialog. Use phrases from Step 1.

Step 5: Play your dialog to the class.

▷ ▪ volunteer ▪ challenge
▪ to lose face ▪ to bully

I can understand some of the problems a foreign boss has.

Vocabulary focus

Focus 1: Two- and three-word phrasal verbs

A Look at these sentences from 1A. Underline the phrasal verbs. Write 2 for two-part verbs and 3 for three-part verbs.

I just don't <u>look forward to</u> coming to work anymore. `3`
I can't get along with the new project manager. ☐
He always seems to <u>find</u> me <u>out</u> at the wrong moment. `2`
The company is trying out a new system. ☐
I can't put up with it any longer. ☐
It's getting me down. ☐
He told me off. ☐
He stormed out of the office. ☐
You can count on me. ☐

The weather is getting me down.

B Match the statements in columns A and B.

A	B
1 I'm a person who **gets along** well **with** everyone. 2 The weather sometimes **gets** me **down**. 3 I can't **put up with** people who are lazy.	`3` Everyone should work as hard as I do. ☐ I don't have any problems with other people. ☐ It depresses me when it's cold and gray.
4 I don't like to be **found out**. 5 My parents often **told** me **off** when I was a kid. 6 I need people that I can **count on**.	☐ I'm lucky to have reliable friends and co-workers. ☐ It's awful when people know I've done something wrong. ☐ Usually because my room was a mess.

C Work with a partner. Which of the statements in column A in 4B are true for you? Add a sentence of your own.

I'm a person who gets along well with everyone (1). I'm always nice and friendly.

D Some phrasal verbs you can separate and some you can't. Put the verbs in these sentences in the right column.

He ~~told~~ me ~~off~~.   You can count on me.   Let's try the new app out.
I take after my father.   Turn the TV off.   What time do you get off work?

Verbs you can separate	Verbs you can't separate
tell off, . . .	. . .

E Use your own ideas to complete the sentences.

1 **A:** Shall I throw away this *leaflet*?
   B: Yes. Throw .... I've read it.

2 **A:** Why do you put up with ....?
   B: I put .... because he's my boss!

3 **A:** It's a bit dark. Shall I turn .... on?
   B: No, don't turn .... I'm sleeping.

4 **A:** Why did you tell .... off?
   B: I told .... because they were noisy.

I can use two- and three-word phrasal verbs.

F Look at the words from 3A. Underline the suffixes.

accept<u>able</u>   peaceful
cultural   sociable
instruction   successful
management   weakness

Sociable people

G Use a verb or an adjective and a suffix to make a noun.
Complete the sentences with the nouns.

Verb or adjective	Suffix	Noun
argue collect ill improve react happy	-ion -ment -ness	**1** Your work shows signs of *improvement*. **2** My co-workers took up a .... for my going-away party. **3** I was surprised by her .... to the news. **4** She returned to work yesterday after a long .... **5** We had a terrible .... and he stormed out. **6** Money can't bring you ....

H Now use a verb or noun and a suffix to make an adjective. Complete the
sentences with the adjectives.

Verb or noun	Suffix	Adjective
profession care origin suit rely power	-able -al -ful	**1** Your clothes are not .... for the office. **2** Be .... you don't delete my files. **3** I can count on my co-workers. They are very .... **4** Could you send me the .... document? **5** Well done. That's a very .... piece of work. **6** China and Russia are .... nations.

I ▷ **Key words** Look at the words at the bottom of pages 27–30. Choose the
best words to complete the sentences.

1 The company asked for .... to
work abroad.
2 I reported a co-worker because
he .... other workers.
3 Please, don't .... me for the
accident. It wasn't my ....
4 The .... department
recruits and trains employees.
5 Stan's new job was a big ....
for him.
6 A person who can't do his job properly
is ....
7 If you .... , you lose
people's respect.
8 The .... among the
co-workers is very good.

*I volunteered. Unemployment
is so bad at the moment.*

I can make nouns and adjectives by using suffixes.

A **Before you read** Work with a partner. Rank these factors for job satisfaction from 1 (most important) to 8 (least important). Then skim the article to see which of the factors it talks about.

☐ boss ☐ challenge ☐ co-workers ☐ flexible working hours
☐ further training ☐ future prospects ☐ job security ☐ money

Asian Business **Online**
looks at job satisfaction throughout the world.

Young and dissatisfied with your job? A new survey shows that young people all over the world are unhappier at work than older people. Many young people said they felt undervalued and underpaid.

Job satisfaction, however, increases with age, and eight out of ten over-50s said they were content with their work. That's hardly surprising – many people that age have already climbed the career ladder, have good positions, and earn a good salary.

Money was in fact ranked as the number one factor for job satisfaction in most of the countries in the survey – which is not surprising as most of us work because we have to pay our bills! After money, job security was the highest factor on the ranking list.

The survey also shows that job satisfaction varies from country to country and from sector to sector. In the United States, the happiest employees can be found in information technology and social services; in Europe, in education and health. Asia reported high satisfaction among workers in the manufacturing, finance, and communication industries.

In the Asia-Pacific region, 68 percent of the employees interviewed ranked their boss as the key factor for job satisfaction or lack of it. Ratana Suttikul, managing director of ABC Employment Services in Thailand, said that many employees wanted further training opportunities, better communication, and more flexible working hours. "Employees often don't leave companies, they leave managers," she said.

The survey shows that the happiest employees in the world are the Canadians: 64 percent said they liked their job, only two percent said work was a necessary evil, and 24 percent said they would work for free!

B **Comprehension** Read the article and answer the questions.

1 Why are many young people unhappy at work?
2 Why are most over-50s content with their work?
3 The survey discovered there are two main factors for job satisfaction. What are they?
4 Where can you find the happiest employees in the
  A education sector? **B** manufacturing sector? **C** social services sector?
5 What do the majority of employees in the Asia-Pacific region want from their bosses?
6 Explain the phrase "a necessary evil."
7 What do the figures refer to?

| eight out of ten | 68 | 24 | 64 |

C **Now you** What is important for you to feel happy and motivated in a job?

boss co-workers job security salary working hours . . .

I can understand an article about job satisfaction.

Business writing
Summaries and reports

A 〔19〕 **Before you listen to the webinar about writing business summaries, put steps A to E in the correct order 1 to 5. Then listen and check.**

A Write sentences based on the parts that you highlighted. ☐
B Read your sentences and make them shorter if possible. ☐
C Read the text quickly for the gist. ☐ 1
D Check that everything is correct. ☐
E Read the text more closely and highlight the important parts. ☐

B 〔19〕 **Listen to the webinar in 6A again and make a summary of the main points.**

- *Before you write, read the text at least twice.*   • Highlight . . .

C **Kim is a business student, and his project is to compare the ASEAN and the EU. Look at the chart. Read the beginning of Kim's report. Complete the report with these phrases and information from the chart.**

| a bit smaller | although | approximately | compared to |
| located in | most used | much larger | was founded |

	ASEAN	EU
Founded	1967	1950s
Size in square kilometers	4.5 million	4.4 million
Member states	10	28
Gross domestic product (GDP)	US$3.6 trillion	US$16 trillion
Population	600 million	500 million
People per square kilometer	135	116
Headquarters	Jakarta	Brussels, Strasbourg, Luxembourg
Working language	English	24 official languages

The Association of Southeast Asian Nations (ASEAN) and the European Union (EU) are political and economic organizations. ASEAN .... in .... and the EU in the 1950s. ASEAN and the EU are .... the same size in square kilometers, but while the EU has .... member states, ASEAN has only ....

The GDP of the EU is .... than that of ASEAN – US$ .... US$3.6 trillion. The population of the EU, however, is quite .... than the population of ASEAN, which stands at about .... with .... people per square kilometer. The EU has a population of about .... with .... people per square kilometer.

ASEAN's headquarters are .... Jakarta. The EU has three .... : one each in Brussels, Strasbourg, and .... ASEAN has only one .... , English. The EU has .... official languages, ... English, French, and German are the working languages ....

D **Choose one of the articles from Asian Business Online in Units 1 to 4. Write a summary. Compare your summary with a partner. Follow the steps in 6A.**

I can understand how to write summaries and reports.

TOEIC® practice

1 Listening

(20) Conversations Listen and answer the questions.

Conversation 1

1 What will the speakers do first?
- ☐ **A** Write the proposal.
- ☐ **B** Discuss the proposal with Ken Tsai.
- ☐ **C** Have lunch.
- ☐ **D** Give the proposal to the director.

2 What will the speakers do last?
- ☐ **A** Write the proposal.
- ☐ **B** Discuss the proposal with Ken Tsai.
- ☐ **C** Have lunch.
- ☐ **D** Give the proposal to the director.

3 Where will the speakers discuss the proposal?
- ☐ **A** In Ken Tsai's office.
- ☐ **B** In the director's office.
- ☐ **C** In the cafeteria.
- ☐ **D** In their office.

Conversation 2

1 What does the woman dislike most about Sandra?
- ☐ **A** She is lazy.
- ☐ **B** She doesn't write down messages.
- ☐ **C** She is getting her down.
- ☐ **D** She tells tales to the boss.

2 What does the man say about Sandra?
- ☐ **A** She is lazy.
- ☐ **B** She is nice.
- ☐ **C** She has changed.
- ☐ **D** She doesn't like her co-workers.

3 What does the man think the best solution would be for the woman?
- ☐ **A** She should ask for a transfer.
- ☐ **B** She should talk to the boss.
- ☐ **C** She should talk to Sandra.
- ☐ **D** She should leave the company.

2 Speaking

Describe a picture Describe the picture in as much detail as possible. You have 30 seconds to prepare your response. Then you have 45 seconds to speak about the picture.

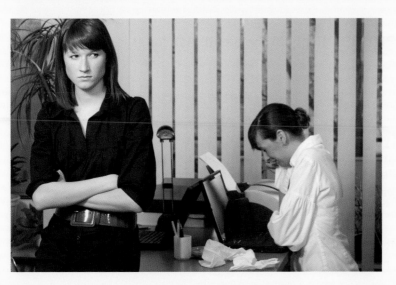

3 Reading

Text completion Read the email. Choose the best word to complete each sentence.

Dear Jill,

Thanks for your email. You asked about the problems I'm having at work. Well, my boss isn't very pleased with me. I was late yesterday and when I arrived at the office, he **1** ....

- [ ] **A** was waiting
- [ ] **B** waited
- [ ] **C** has waited
- [ ] **D** waits

for me. He was really angry and he **2** ....

- [ ] **A** told off me.
- [ ] **B** did tell me off.
- [ ] **C** told me off.
- [ ] **D** did tell off me.

He said that it **3** .... the third time this month that I was late.

- [ ] **A** were
- [ ] **B** was
- [ ] **C** be
- [ ] **D** has been

He told me **4** .... harder to be punctual, or I might lose my job!

- [ ] **A** I tried
- [ ] **B** I try
- [ ] **C** trying
- [ ] **D** to try

Best wishes,
Max

4 Writing

Respond to a written request Reply to the email. Ask for at least TWO more pieces of information.

Dear Sir or Madam:

I saw an advertisement for your personal assistant service on the Internet. I am a professional woman, married with two children, and I am interested in finding help to organize my busy life. I would like to know more about the baby-sitting service you offer and your prices.

Sincerely,
Ms. Mary Murphy

Getting your message across

1 Business situation
Communication media

A |21| Peter Hansen is the Asia sales manager for a textile company in Manchester, UK. Listen to his conversation with his assistant, Donna Shrimpton. They mention five different ways of communicating. What are they?

B |21| Listen again. Who says . . . ? Write *P* for Peter or *D* for Donna.

1 I need to know when you're available.   D
2 I had planned to work from home on Thursday.   ....
3 Do you have access to Skype at home?   ....
4 Thank goodness for technology.   ....
5 Maybe you sent it to the wrong person.   ....
6 I had a (. . .) stopover in Singapore.   ....
7 People aren't cautious enough.   ....
8 Check before you click send.   ....

C |21| Listen again and answer the questions.

1 How and when will the meeting with the Thailand office take place?
2 Where was Peter when he sent his wife a text message, and what was he doing there?
3 What went wrong with Peter's text message?
4 How did Peter's friend react to the message?
5 What is Donna's opinion of Peter's technology skills?

D **Now you** Work with a partner. Make a list of the advantages and disadvantages of each communication medium you listed in 1A. Compare your list with another pair.

▷ ▪ available ▪ access ▪ stopover
▪ cautious ▪ state-of-the-art

I can understand a conversation about communication media.

Grammar focus
Focus 1: Past perfect

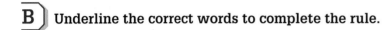

A Look at the sentences from 1A. Which tense are the verbs?

1 the simple past *(did)*?
2 the past perfect *(had done)*?

I **texted** ☐1 her because she **hadn't replied** ☐ to my email.
She **said** ☐ she **hadn't received** ☐ it.
I **realized** ☐ I**'d sent** ☐ the text to the wrong person!

Hi, darling,
I'm on my way.
C U soon.

B Underline the correct words to complete the rule.

We form the past perfect with **has** / **had** + the past participle. We use the past perfect to describe an action that took place **before** / **after** another action or a time in the past.

Don't confuse the short forms:

I'd sent it to the wrong person. (= had)

If I were you, I'd send it again. (= would)

C Complete the sentences. Use the two verbs in brackets, one in the simple past and one in the past perfect.

1 When I *had written* (write) the report, I *went* (go) to lunch.
2 I .... (try) to email Anocha, but she .... (close) down her computer.
3 When Tom .... (leave) the company, he .... (work) there for five years.
4 We .... (not end) the meeting until we .... (decide) on a strategy.
5 I really .... (enjoy) dinner because I .... (not eat) all day.
6 Donna .... (introduce) us because we .... (not meet) before.
7 As soon as I .... (prepare) my presentation, I .... (go) to the meeting.
8 I .... (call) Anocha about the meeting, but she .... (leave) the office.

D Complete the sentences with your own ideas. Use the verbs in brackets and the past perfect.

She hadn't switched
her phone off.

1 My phone rang during the movie because
I hadn't switched it off. (not switch off)
2 I had to rewrite the report because .... (make)
3 I missed the flight because .... (forget)
4 I couldn't go to the concert because .... (not book)
5 I lost my way to his office because ....
(misunderstand)
6 My boss was very angry because .... (miss)
7 I already knew the Thai co-workers because ....
(talk)
8 I didn't have time for lunch because .... (not finish)

I can talk about past events using the past perfect.

Grammar focus

Focus 2: Review of present and past tenses

E Which of the descriptions 1 to 6 matches the letters A to F? Write the letters.

1 An action in progress in the past. ☐
2 An action that started and finished before another action or a time in the past. ☐
3 An action in progress now. ☐
4 An action that started and finished at a time in the past. ☐
5 An action in a time that is not yet finished. ☐
6 An action that happens usually or often. ☐

Tense	Description	Example with *he + work*
Present simple	6	*he works*
Present continuous		
Past continuous		
Past simple		
Present perfect		
Past perfect		

F Match the sentence parts.

1 My co-worker helps me	B	A so I can finish the report today.
2 My co-worker is helping me	A	B whenever I ask her to.

3 I had fixed the printer,	....	A so I printed some handouts.
4 I was fixing the printer	....	B when I cut my hand.

5 They worked in this company	....	A many years ago.
6 They have worked in this company	....	B since 2012.

7 I first met Peter Hansen	....	A when he visits our company.
8 I have often met Peter Hansen	....	B when he visited our company.

9 Donna hasn't finish her work,	....	A so she has to stay longer in the office.
10 Donna hadn't finished her work,	....	B so I waited for her.

11 I was working hard	....	A all day yesterday.
12 I worked hard	....	B when Tom called.

G Work with a partner. Choose a time of day and take turns to ask and answer questions.

1 What do you usually do at *eight o'clock in the evening*?
   — *I usually do yoga.*
2 What were you doing at ....?
3 What did you do after that?
4 What had you done before ....?

I can use the present and past tenses.

Listening and speaking
Business news

A How do you find out about the news – the Internet, TV, radio, newspapers? What are the advantages and disadvantages of each medium?

B What kind of news (sports? business?) interests you the most and why?

C [22] Listen to the Asia-Pacific business news. Match the countries 1 to 4 to the news headlines A to D.

1 Japan	....	**A** Record price
2 Singapore	....	**B** Development plans
3 Malaysia	....	**C** Record-breaking company
4 Australia	....	**D** Positive developments in the labor market

D [22] Listen again and decide if the statements are true, false, or not stated. Correct the false statements.

	True	False	Not stated
1 The unemployment rate in Japan has decreased.	☐	☐	☐
2 There are more jobs than job seekers in Japan.	☐	☐	☐
3 Changi airport handled 4.5 million passengers in one month.	☐	☐	☐
4 The Changi Airport Group made a profit last year.	☐	☐	☐
5 Passenger numbers have increased by 11 percent since last May.	☐	☐	☐
6 The Malaysian government is planning to build a duty-free shopping center close to the Malaysia-Thailand border.			
7 Thousands of Thais cross the border to shop every day.	☐	☐	☐
8 The Bank of New South Wales opened in 1870.	☐	☐	☐
9 The ten-shilling note was found in Sydney.	☐	☐	☐

E Talking about ... news stories

Student A: Look at Partner file 3.
Student B: Look at Partner file 4.

Step 1: Read the news article in your Partner file and make a note of the main points. Give your partner a summary of your story.

Step 2: Listen to your partner's summary of his/her news story and ask questions for further details.

Step 3: Find an interesting local news story and summarize it.

Step 4: Work in small groups and tell each other your stories.

▷ ▪ unemployment ▪ to recruit ▪ job seeker
▪ auction ▪ raw materials

I can listen to and summarize business news stories.

Vocabulary focus
Focus 1: Compound nouns and adjectives

A Look at these compound nouns and adjectives from the conversation in 1A. Read the transcript on pages 104–105 and find another example of each.

A two-hour delay

Compound nouns	Compound adjectives
videoconference stopover	nonstop two-hour ....

> Some compound nouns are written as one word *(boyfriend)*, some as two words *(post office)*, and some with a hyphen *(baby-sitter)*. Use a dictionary to check.

B Compound nouns or compound adjectives? Make a chart like in 4A.

brand-new   businessman   computer virus   credit card   fifteen-year-old
first-class   job seeker   movie star   part-time   phone number
second-hand   smartphone   state-of-the-art   time zone   traffic jam
travel agent   T-shirt   twenty-minute   website   world-famous

> Compound adjectives have a hyphen when they come *before* a noun.
> *It's a well-known brand.   The brand is well known.*

C (23) Listen to the compound nouns. Which word is stressed?

D Replace the underlined words with a compound word from 4A and 4B.
1 The equipment is completely new. *brand new*
2 I'm looking for job where I can work half a day.
3 We took a direct flight to Tokyo.
4 The team members all work in different regions where the time is the same.
5 I got stuck in a long line of cars and missed the flight.
6 In my company we work with the most modern and up-to-date technology.
7 I booked my vacation with a person who organizes trips.
8 There are more people who are looking for a job than jobs.

E Find a suitable noun to follow the compound adjective.
1 We arrived late because there was a two-hour *delay*.
2 Peter stayed in a three-star .... in Bangkok.
3 I found a well-paid .... after I graduated from college.
4 You can go on foot. It's about a fifteen-minute ....
5 We took a nonstop .... to Bangkok.
6 Sunan handed in a well-written ....
7 Richard Branson is a world-famous ....
8 It was a very badly organized ....

A ten-dollar bill

> *I can* use compound nouns and adjectives.

Vocabulary focus
Focus 2: Opinions, agreeing, and disagreeing

F Look at the phrases below. Which phrases are used to . . .

1 ask for an opinion?   **2** give an opinion?   **3** agree?   **4** disagree?

I'm afraid I can't agree. ☐	Absolutely! ☐	If you ask me . . . ☐
How do you see it? ☐	I couldn't agree more. ☐	Sorry, I disagree. ☐
I'd like to hear your view. ☐	In my opinion, . . . ☐	You're absolutely right. ☐
I suppose you're right. ☐	That's true. ☐	What do you think? ☐

When we say something another person may not like, use:

Sorry, I disagree.

I'm afraid I've deleted the file.

CAREER ADVISER

If you want people to think you are clever, agree with them.

G Say the sentences in another way. Use the words on the right.

1 I think videoconferencing is the cheapest way to have meetings.	*opinion*
2 I have a different opinion than you about videoconferencing.	*disagree*
3 I'd like to hear your opinion.	*think*
4 I definitely have the same opinion as you about communication media.	*agree*
5 What do you think about it?	*see*

H Work in groups of four. You all work for a Japanese company, but you live in different Asian countries. You are planning to work on a project together and are having an informal meeting in Tokyo to discuss the best way to communicate.

Listen to the others' opinions and give yours. Use some of the phrases from 4F.

Student A: Look at Partner file 5.   Student C: Look at Partner file 7.
Student B: Look at Partner file 6.   Student D: Look at the information below.

You live in Tokyo in Japan. You would like team meetings at your company's headquarters in Tokyo at least once a month, backed up by emailing and telephoning. You are not a friend of new technologies. You don't like videoconferencing because the camera makes you nervous. You don't like the idea of shared digital workspace, where all communication and information sharing is done online, as that would be completely new for you.

I ▷ **Key words** Look at the words at the bottom of pages 37–40. Choose the best words to complete the sentences.

1 I will let you have .... to my computer files.
2 It wasn't a direct flight. We had a(n) .... in Dubai.
3 Things are sold at a(n) .... to the person who offers the highest price.
4 There is high .... when there are more .... than jobs.
5 As a result of the good economic situation, companies .... more staff.
6 .... such as coal and metals are needed for production.
7 The control panel on the latest model uses .... - .... - .... - .... technology.
8 "..................." means "extremely careful".

I can ask for and give opinions, agree, and disagree.

Reading
Speak like an American

A **Before you read** Work in small groups. Do you know any differences between American English and British English? Make a list. Compare your list with another group.

Asian Business **Online**
looks at the U.S.-English boom in Hong Kong.

Hong Kong was a British colony for 156 years, and English is still widely taught and spoken there today. But a growing number of children – some of them as young as five – prefer to learn American rather than British English.

When Mike Yan opened the Broadway School of English ten years ago, he had only 40 pupils. Today he has 340. "The increase," he says, "is partly because American culture has become mainstream. Most students have watched Hollywood films and popular TV dramas, and that makes a U.S. accent easier for them to understand and copy."

According to Mr. Yan, an American accent is seen to be "more modern and more international," while both British and American accents suggest that someone comes from a good background and can afford to study abroad.

"I intend to send my sons to university in the United States, so it's better if they have an American accent," says David Yu, whose sons Benny, aged eight, and Sam, six, attend the Broadway School. "I think that an American accent will give them more job opportunities in the West."

A lot of students now come from mainland China. "When we first opened, we had zero students from the mainland, but now about 30 percent are from there. We expect that number to grow as more and more people can afford to pay for private education for their children," says Mr. Yan.

"Some people still prefer the British accent," Dr. Victor Li, an English teacher at City University, told Asian Business Online. "I believe that the Hong Kongers' fondness for the United Kingdom means a British accent will remain popular."

B **The main idea** Which sentence gives the main idea of the text? A, B, or C?

A A British English accent has a negative image in Hong Kong.
B An American English accent has a positive image in Hong Kong.
C English language schools are very important in Hong Kong.

C **Comprehension** Read the text and answer the questions.

1 Who is: **A** Mike Yan? **B** David Yu? **C** Victor Li?
2 How many reasons can you find in the article for the popularity of a US accent in Hong Kong? What are they?

D **Meaning in context** Find these words in the text. Can you guess their meaning? How did you guess?

| widely taught | mainstream | according to | mainland | fondness |

E **Now you**

1 Name three languages you think are important to learn. Give reasons.
2 Are there different accents in your language? Which are more/less popular?

I can understand an article about English accents.

Culture focus
Business cultures

A Study these "word clouds." Check that you know the meanings of the words. Discuss the differences with a partner:

In high-context culture . . . is important, but in low-context culture . . .

High-context business culture

Examples: China, Japan, Korea, Latin America, Saudi Arabia

Low-context business culture

Examples: the United States, most northern European countries

B 【24】 Now listen to two speakers talking about business cultures in their countries. What kind of cultures do they each come from?

Speaker 1	☐ high-context	☐ low-context
Speaker 2	☐ high-context	☐ low-context

C One of the pairs of sentences is typical of a high-context culture (write *H*) and one of a low-context culture (write *L*). Give reasons for your answers.

1 **A** You have my word. H
  B Could you put that in writing? L
  In low-context cultures people want things in writing. In high-context cultures you have to trust your business partner.

2 **A** I need more information before I can make a decision. ☐
  B I just have the feeling that he's the right person for the job. ☐

3 **A** I don't think that's allowed. ☐
  B You shouldn't do that. ☐

4 **A** Teamwork is very important. ☐
  B I prefer to solve my problems myself. ☐

5 **A** I don't understand what you are saying. ☐
  B Could you explain that to me again, please? ☐

6 **A** My staff need feedback – positive and negative. ☐
  B My staff know when I am pleased or not. I don't need to say anything. ☐

Teamwork

D Describe your culture with words from the word clouds in 6A.

> *I can* understand some differences between business cultures.

1 Business situation
Planning an international conference

A 〔25〕 Rob March is head of sales at an international company based in Jakarta. He and his co-workers are having a meeting to plan an international conference. Listen to the conversation. Mark (✗) what they do NOT talk about.

- [ ] accommodations
- [ ] budget
- [ ] location
- [ ] mailing list
- [ ] program
- [ ] promotion
- [ ] registration
- [ ] speakers
- [ ] technical requirements
- [ ] translating service
- [ ] venue

B 〔25〕 Listen again and answer the questions.

1 What kind of rooms do they need for the conference?
2 What other facilities must the venue have? Name three things.
3 What do these figures refer to?
   2,000   60   5   3   6
4 What has each of them already done?
   A Dinda   **B** Akmal   **C** Nuri

C 〔25〕 Who says what? Write *R* for Rob, *D* for Dinda, *N* for Nuri, *A* for Akmal, and *J* for Jed.

1 Let's get started. ....
2 Would you like to begin? ....
3 Let's move on to the next point. ....
4 Can I interrupt there? ....
5 Just let me finish, please. ....
6 Are you with me? ....
7 Can we get back to the main point? ....
8 I'll take care of that. ....
9 Are you saying that . . . ? ....

▷ ▪ venue ▪ facility ▪ shuttle service
▪ to require ▪ requirement

I can understand a conversation about planning a conference.

Grammar focus

Focus 1: Review of *going to* and *will*-future

A Look at sentences 1 to 3 and match them with definitions A to C.

1 I'll help you to do some research.	**A** a prediction for the future
2 I'm going to choose the three best.	**B** a definite plan for the future
3 I think we'll need six weeks.	**C** spontaneous offer or promise

B Decide which definition (A, B, or C) from 2A matches these sentences.

1 Dinda, you're going to check out the venue.   B
2 I'll bear in mind your favorite sport.   ....
3 Most people will arrive by air.   ....
4 Who's going to organize the workshop registrations?   ....
5 I'll take care of that.   ....
6 I'll probably update last year's registration form.   ....
7 Participants will have to book their flights.   ....
8 We're going to invite some new speakers.   ....

C How would you react to these statements? Use the words in brackets and *I'll*.

1 I don't know how to get to Jed's office. (the way)
   I'll show you the way.
2 The telephone is ringing. (answer)
3 It's Dinda's birthday. (flowers)
4 Could you tell Rob I'll be late? (text message)
5 I have to leave now. (coat)
6 I feel a bit tired. (coffee)
7 It's cold in this room. (heat)
8 It's warm in this room. (window)
9 Are the figures correct? (check)
10 I forgot to bring my camera. (lend)

> We say: *Yes, I will* to say we can do something.
> *No, I won't* is impolite. If we can't do it, we say: *I'm afraid I can't.*

D Complete the sentences. Use the verbs in brackets with *will* or *going to*.

1 Dinda has put an advertisement on eBay. She .... (sell) her car.
2 **A:** I'm afraid I'm not ready.
   B: That's OK. I .... (wait).
3 I'm on the Singapore Airlines website. I .... (book) a flight.
4 The conference .... (probably be) in Vietnam this year.
5 I've downloaded the app because I .... (practice) my English.
6 **A:** Sorry the line is busy.
   B: No problem. I .... (hold).
7 Is my car blocking your way? Sorry. I ....
   (move) it immediately.
8 **A:** I .... (have) lunch at the sushi bar.
   B: Good idea! I .... (come) with you.

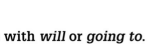

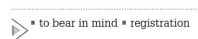
▸ ▪ to bear in mind ▪ registration

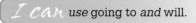
I can use going to *and* will.

E 🔊 **25** Listen to the conversation in 1A again. Complete the sentences in reported speech.

	Direct speech	Reported speech
Commands and advice	"Remember to keep an eye on the costs."	Rob **reminded** Dinda to .... an eye on the costs.
	"Please quote us a price."	Dinda **asked** the hotels to .... them a price.
	"Put together a mailing list."	Akmal **told** the sales department ....
	"You should check the speakers' technical requirements.	Rob **advised** Nuri ....
Yes/No questions	"Do you want to prepare the program?"	Rob **asked** Nuri if she ....
	"Can you come again this year?"	Nuri **asked** the speakers whether they ....

F Complete the rule.

When we report . . .
• advice and commands, the reporting verb is followed by an object + ... + verb.
• questions, we use *if* or .... and change the present tense to the .... tense.

G Dinda contacted five venues to get information. Later she told her co-workers what she had said. What did she tell them?

1 *I asked them if they had a conference room for 60 participants.*

1 Do you have a conference room for 60 participants?

2 Can you offer state-of-the-art technical facilities?

3 Do you provide a shuttle service?

4 Please, tell us your deadline for final bookings.

5 You should send an offer as soon as possible.

6 Quote me a price by email.

7 Don't forget to send a restaurant menu with the offer.

8 Do you need any more details?

Note the position of *not*:
He told me <u>not</u> to spend too much money.

I can report questions, advice, and commands.

A 〔26〕 **Listen to the end of the meeting in 1A. Choose the correct answer.**

1 Who is responsible for team-building activities?
- [ ] **A** Jed
- [ ] **B** Nuri
- [ ] **C** Akmal

2 Who is going to research the venue?
- [ ] **A** Dinda and Akmal
- [ ] **B** Dinda and Jed
- [ ] **C** Dinda and Nuri

3 Who is going to organize the interpreters?
- [ ] **A** Dinda
- [ ] **B** Nuri
- [ ] **C** nobody

4 Rob asked Nuri to put the action points . . .
- [ ] **A** in the agenda.
- [ ] **B** in the minutes.
- [ ] **C** in an email.

5 Everyone will receive the minutes . . .
- [ ] **A** at the end of the week.
- [ ] **B** today.
- [ ] **C** tomorrow morning.

6 What should everyone bring to the next meeting?
- [ ] **A** research results
- [ ] **B** action points
- [ ] **C** some good ideas

B 〔26〕 **Listen to the conversation again. Check (✔) the phrases you hear.**

- [ ] I think we've covered everything.
- [ ] Are there any other questions?
- [ ] I have one more question.
- [ ] We're running out of time.
- [ ] I'd like to summarize.
- [ ] Let me sum up.
- [ ] The last item on the agenda is AOB.
- [ ] I'll go over the main points again.
- [ ] The meeting is closed.
- [ ] Thank you for coming.

C **Talking about ...** a class excursion

You are going to have a meeting to plan a class excursion.

Step 1: Work with a partner. Think of all the points you need to discuss (date, location, type of excursion, transportation arrangements, how the work of preparation will be shared, . . .).

Step 2: Now work in small groups. Compare your lists and draft an agenda for the meeting.

Step 3: Hold the meeting. Choose a chairperson and an agenda. Use the phrases from 1C and 3B. Everyone should take notes about the decisions the group makes.

▷ ▪ interpreter ▪ action point
▪ team building ▪ excursion

I can take part in a meeting.

4 Vocabulary focus
The language of meetings

A Look at phrases A to H. Which phrase can you use to . . .

1 begin a meeting? ....
2 ask for agreement? ....
3 return to the main topic? ....
4 go on to another topic? ....
5 interrupt? ....
6 stop an interruption? ....
7 sum up? ....
8 check understanding? ....

A Can I interrupt there?	**E** Just let me finish, please.
B Are you with me?	**F** I'd like to summarize.
C Let's get started.	**G** Can we get back to the main point?
D Let's move on to the next point.	**H** Don't you think so?

B Put the words in the correct order. Then check your answers in the transcripts to 1A and 3A on pages 106–107.

1 last / agenda / is / on / the / AOB / the / item .
2 we've / think / everything / covered / I .
3 let's / point / on / the / take / the / agenda / first .
4 time / we're / out / of / running .
5 like / I'd /summarize / points / to / the / action .
6 I / come/ there / just / in /may ?
7 begin / you / like / to / would ?
8 if /else / the / meeting / is / nothing / there's / to / closed / discuss .

C Find the phrases in 4B.

1 two phrases used at the beginning of a meeting
2 five phrases used at the end of a meeting
3 one phrase used to interrupt

D Which is the odd word out?

1 **take**	☐ the minutes	☐ notes	☒ the agenda	
2 **do**	☐ a presentation	☐ a meeting	☐ a project	
3 **make**	☐ an action point	☐ an arrangement	☐ a decision	
4 **choose**	☐ a venue	☐ the minutes	☐ a chairperson	
5 **reject**	☐ an interruption	☐ a suggestion	☐ a conference	
6 **prepare**	☐ an arrangement	☐ the agenda	☐ a conference room	
7 **update**	☐ a registration form	☐ a mailing list	☐ a workshop	
8 **give**	☐ a speech	☐ an explanation	☐ an agreement	
9 **cover**	☐ a meeting	☐ an item	☐ a topic	
10 **hire**	☐ a venue	☐ a leisure program	☐ an interpreter	

To BEGIN WITH, I'D LIKE TO APOLOGIZE FOR MY BEHAVIOR AT OUR RECENT MEETING!

E Complete the text with words from 4D in the correct form.

At the second meeting two weeks later, Rob was the c................
again and Nuri t................ the m................ The first i................
on the a................ was the v................ for the sales c................
Dinda d................ a p................ of the three hotels she had
c................ Jed tried to interrupt, but Dinda r................ the
i................ She asked again about h................ translators and
i................ , but Rob repeated that they were too expensive.
Then it was Akmal's turn. He explained that he had u................
the r................ f................ and p................ the mailing list. Jed talked
about the leisure program, but Rob r................ some of his s................ and
reminded everyone of the budget. After they had c........... everything on the agenda,
Rob g................ a short s................ He summarized the new a................
p................ and made an a................ for the next meeting.

INTERPRETERS

#!@%*

An *interpreter* translates spoken language;
a *translator* translates written language.

F Complete the chart with your ideas. Discuss your answers with a partner.

In a meeting . . .			In American culture	In your culture
1	when somebody is speaking, you	A look the person in the eye. B look at your papers. C look around the room.	A	
2	if you want to interrupt, you	A start to speak immediately. B wait for a pause and use a polite phrase. C put up your hand and stand up.		
3	if you shake your head, it shows	A you are angry. B you agree. C you disagree.		

G ▷ **Key words** Look at the words at the bottom of pages 45–48. Choose the best words to complete the sentences.

1 I couldn't speak Chinese, so I hired a(n) ....
2 Please .... that we must keep to the budget.
3 There's a good .... from the hotel to the airport.
4 Does the hotel have all the .... that we .... ?
5 None of the .... meets our ....
6 The company is planning a(n) .... to Bali.
7 A(n) .... is something that must be done after a meeting.
8 Please send us your .... form before March 31.

I can understand and use the language of meetings.

Presentations

1 Business situation
The dos and don'ts of presentations

A 〔29〕 Nicole Shaw is giving a training session on presentations in an international company in Singapore. Before you listen, decide which of these ideas will be "dos" and which will be "don'ts." Then listen and check (✔) the advice you hear.

		Do	Don't
1	Research your topic carefully.	☐	☐
2	Write down everything you want to say.	☐	☐
3	Make sure the technical equipment has been checked.	☐	☐
4	Read from your notes.	☐	☐
5	Tell some jokes.	☐	☐
6	Give your audience "signposts."	☐	☐
7	Speak slowly.	☐	☐
8	Let the audience interrupt with questions.	☐	☐
9	Dress professionally.	☐	☐
10	Avoid direct eye contact with the audience.	☐	☐

B 〔29〕 Listen again and answer the questions.

1 How does Nicole Shaw start her presentation?
2 Besides presentations, what are the other top five fears?
3 Nicole Shaw's presentation has four parts. What are they?
4 Why should you give "signposts"?
5 What does Nicole mean by "the right clothes"?
6 How does Nicole close her presentation?

▷ ▪ to distribute ▪ signpost ▪ to underestimate
▪ casual ▪ dress code

I can understand how to give a presentation.

Grammar focus
Focus 1: The passive

A Put the verb tenses A and B in the column on the left. Then complete the passive sentences. Read the transcript for the presentation in 1A on page 108 and check.

A Present continuous   **B** Present perfect

Tense	Active	Passive
....	**1** Make sure somebody **has prepared** the room and **has checked** the equipment.	Make sure the room........................ .... and the technical equipment ....
....	**2** Don't block the view when you **are showing** visuals.	Don't block the view when visuals ....!

B What did the people say in these situations? Make passive sentences with the words in brackets.

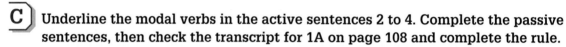

1 My phone is missing. (I hope / it / not / steal)
    I hope it hasn't been stolen.
2 The co-workers are in the seminar room. (they / train / by Nicole)
3 Your office looks different. (the walls / paint ?)
4 The photocopier is working again. (it / repair / yesterday)
5 This company is big. (300 people / employ /here)
6 There were three applicants for the job. (they / interview / right now)

C Underline the modal verbs in the active sentences 2 to 4. Complete the passive sentences, then check the transcript for 1A on page 108 and complete the rule.

Active	Passive
1 You *must* photocopy handouts in advance.	Handouts *must be photocopied* in advance.
2 Speak loudly enough so that everyone can hear and understand you.	Speak loudly enough so that you .... and .... by everyone.
3 You should save questions for the end of your talk.	Questions .... for the end of your talk.
4 People might not take you seriously.	You .... seriously.

The passive infinitive after modal verbs is formed with *be* + ...

D Change the sentences into the passive. Use the modal verb in brackets.

1 Don't make appointments before next week. (can) *Appointments can be made next week.*
2 Solve the problem soon! (must) ....
3 Don't make a decision before the next meeting. (should) ....
4 Postpone the meeting until next month. (can) ....
5 Do something before it's too late. (should) ....
6 Don't make the same mistake again. (must) ....

▷ • handout • appearance
    • to postpone

I can use the passive in different tenses and with modal verbs.

Grammar focus
Focus 2: *So* and *such*

E Look at the statements Nicole Shaw made in her presentation and underline the correct words in the rule below.

1 It's no wonder speakers get **so** nervous.
2 It's **so** important to research your topic carefully.
3 It's **such an** easy thing to forget.
4 It's **such a** common mistake.

> If we want to make the meaning of an adjective stronger, we use:
> **so** / **such** + adjective
> **so** / **such** + *a(n)* + adjective + noun

F Complete the sentences with *so* or *such a(n)*.

1 It was *such a* long presentation and I was *so* bored.
2 The new equipment was .... expensive, but it was .... big improvement.
3 This job is .... hard and there's .... much to do.
4 Bangkok is .... great city and it's .... exciting.
5 My co-workers are .... nice. We're .... good team.
6 My boss is .... nice person and .... good boss.
7 .... lot of people have a smartphone now because they are .... cheap.

I was so bored.

G [30] Listen to the sentences from 2F. Notice the extra stress on *so* and *such*. Listen again and repeat the sentences.

H Make one sentence from two. Use *so* or *such* and *that* if necessary.

1 ~~Lisa was a hard worker.~~	I'll have to work late tonight.
2 My English is bad.	We really enjoyed ourselves.
3 I have a lot to do.	~~She was soon promoted.~~
4 Chen was tired.	I need to practice more.
5 My country is beautiful.	Not many foreigners try to learn it.
6 It was a great party.	You should come and visit.
7 I didn't realize it was late.	It's time for me to go.
8 Chinese is a difficult language.	He fell asleep during the meeting.

Lisa was such a hard worker (that) she was soon promoted.

I Make sentences about yourself. Tell a partner.

1 I like . . . because it's so . . .
  I like Tokyo because it's so exciting.
2 I don't like . . . because it's so . . .
3 I like . . . because it's such a . . .
4 I don't like . . . because it's such a . . .
5 I wish I wasn't so . . .
6 I wish I hadn't gotten such a . . .
7 I wouldn't like to be a(n) . . . It's so . . .

Such a big sandwich!

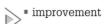
▪ improvement

> *I can* use so and such.

A) **[31]** The students at Nicole Shaw's training session each gave a presentation. Listen to the feedback other students gave to Chen Ming after his presentation. What was good about the presentation and what was not so good?

B) **[31]** Listen again and decide if the statements are true, false, or not stated. Correct the false statements.

	True	False	Not stated
1 Chen had never given a presentation before.	☐	☐	☐
2 Suling thinks Chen didn't do enough research.	☐	☐	☐
3 Luke enjoyed the visuals.	☐	☐	☐
4 Nicole Shaw doesn't agree that Chen spoke too fast.	☐	☐	☐
5 Chen forgot to give signposts in his presentation.	☐	☐	☐
6 Chen spent a lot of time preparing his presentation.	☐	☐	☐
7 Chen appreciated the feedback.	☐	☐	☐
8 Chen's presentation was the best one in the group.	☐	☐	☐

C) Talking about ... good and bad presentations

Step 1: Complete the sentences and then compare your answers with a partner.

1 "Signpost" the structure of your presentation so that your audience . . .
2 Give lots of examples in order to . . .
3 Use visuals because . . .
4 Save questions for the end of your talk so that . . .
5 Aim to dress professionally so that . . .
6 The more you practice, the . . .

HOW TO GIVE A SUCCESSFUL PRESENTATION

Step 2: With a partner make a list of what might go wrong or you might do wrong in a presentation.

Step 3: Compare your lists with another pair. Brainstorm the best solution to each problem.

Step 4: Make a class list on the board of problems and solutions. Copy the lists into your notebook.

▷ ▪ to race through ▪ to structure
   ▪ eye contact ▪ on the whole

I can *understand and talk about what makes a good presentation.*

4 Vocabulary focus

Focus 1: The language of presentations

A 〔32〕 **Listen to parts of Nicole Shaw's presentation and fill in the blanks.**

1 My name is Nicole Shaw and I'm here today to .... what makes a good presentation.
2 I'm going to .... into four parts.
3 .... to talk about planning and preparation. .... will be about opening your presentation and some tips on giving the presentation itself. .... I'll give you some ideas for closing your presentation.
4 ...., I'd like to talk about clothes and body language.
5 .... with planning and preparation.
6 .... the end of my presentation. Thank you for ....
7 Now, if anyone has any questions, I'll do ....

B **Put the parts of a presentation in the correct order.**

☐ **A** So, that's all we have time for today. Are there any questions?
☐ **B** Then I'll move on to the advantages of the product compared with others on the market.
1 **C** Good morning. My name is David Choo and my subject today is the new presentation software package that my company is putting on the market.
☐ **D** My presentation is going to be in three main parts.
☐ **E** First, I'll demonstrate the software package itself and its special features.
☐ **F** OK. Now, let's start by looking at the product. Here you can see . . .
☐ **G** Thank you for coming today and thank you for your attention.
☐ **H** Finally, I'll talk about prices and delivery times.
☐ **I** Before we finish, I'd just like to sum up.

C **In pairs, prepare a five-minute presentation on one of the topics in the word cloud. Use the structure below and phrases from 4A and 4B. Decide who will do each step and give your presentation.**

the ideal job
vacations a place I would like to work
college **a product**
a sport *social media*
social media COLLEGE vacations
a product **how to . . .**
vacations *COLLEGE*
a sport career plans
a place I would like to work
the ideal job
vacations

How to structure a presentation

Step 1: Introduce yourself and the topic.

Step 2: Tell listeners how many parts the presentation will have and what they will be.

Step 3: Give the main body of the presentation using "signposts" to guide your listeners.

Step 4: Sum up.

Step 5: Thank listeners and give them the opportunity to ask questions.

Step 6: Close the presentation.

I can use the language of presentations.

D Look at the sentences. Are the nouns in bold followed by singular or plural verbs? Make a chart, then compare your ideas with a partner.

The **advice** Nicole gave us was very useful.
Professional **clothes** are important.
The designer **jeans** I bought were very expensive.
Dark **pants** are more formal than jeans.
A lot of **information** is collected online.
I'm sorry, but the **news** is not very good.
My **luck** has changed.
Her new **glasses** look really nice.
Economics was my best subject in college.
These **scissors** are not very sharp.

Her glasses are new.

Always singular + singular verb	Always plural + plural verb	Look plural but + singular verb
advice . . .	*clothes . . .*	*economics . . .*

With quantities we use a singular verb:

Twenty kilometers is a long way to walk.

A million dollars is a lot of money.

E There are mistakes in some of these sentences. Spot the mistakes and correct them.

We don't use *a* or *an* with the words in 4D. We use *a pair of*, *a piece of*, or *some*:

a pair of jeans, *a piece of* news, *some* advice

1 Some of the informations you gave me were wrong.
2 I want to buy a new pair of jeans.
3 Three weeks weren't enough vacation.
4 That news don't make me very happy.
5 Could you pass me those scissors, please?
6 Let me give you an advice.
7 Two thousand dollars is a good salary.
8 Do you only have one pants with you?

F ▷ **Key words** Look at the words at the bottom of pages 55–58. Choose the best words to complete the sentences.

1 .... will be .... by the speaker at the end of the presentation.
2 The .... in our company is relaxed and we all wear .... clothes.
3 You can use .... to show the structure of your presentation.
4 Why was the meeting .... until tomorrow?
5 Slow down and don't .... your presentation.
6 .... the meeting went very well.
7 Don't .... the importance of appearance.
8 Smile and make .... with your listeners.

I can use singular and plural nouns.

Cosmetics-for-men craze in South Korea

A) Before you read Talk to a partner. Do men in your country use cosmetics? What do they use? Skim the article to see if any of those items are mentioned.

Asian Business **Online**

looks at the importance of appearance in the business world.

More cosmetics than ever before are being used by South Korean men as the need to look good reaches the workplace. Five years ago, South Korean men spent $500 million a year on cosmetics. Today, the figure is $900 million – by far the fastest growing market for men's cosmetics!

Korean Air's staff training sessions at Incheon International Airport now include makeup and skin-care lessons for male staff. "More and more modern men are realizing the importance of appearance in the workplace and in the job market," says spokesperson Park Su-hyun, "A good first impression is essential."

The biggest demand is for skin-care products, but the market is rapidly expanding to include makeup, and South Korea has become the makeup capital of the world. "Appearance is power," says Kim Yong-ha, a 23-year-old college student who regularly wears lipstick and uses a black pencil to color his eyebrows. "I feel more confident when I wear makeup. We see how great Korean pop stars look, and we want to look like them."

Walk into any cosmetics store in Seoul and you will find a men's section where you can buy anything from anti-age creams to mascara. Cosmetic studios and beauty spas for men are springing up everywhere, and men are regularly spending $200 to $400 on a beauty treatment. TV shows telling men how to make the best of themselves attract thousands of viewers, and there is a new term, a "Grooming Joe," to describe a man who is willing to invest in beauty products.

However, research analysts predict that while China will overtake South Korea in market size for men's cosmetics in the next few years, South Korea will keep the top place in terms of per-capita spending. It seems that South Korean men think they are worth it.

B) Scanning for detail Are the statements correct? If not, correct them.

1 South Korean men spend almost twice as much on cosmetics as they did five years ago.
2 The article tells us that modern men are using cosmetics to please their girlfriends.
3 Park Su-hyun is a research analyst.
4 South Korean men buy more makeup than skin-care products.
5 Kim Yong-ha wants to look like a pop star.
6 Men often spend $200 to $400 in cosmetics stores.
7 Grooming Joe is a man with a TV show that attracts thousands of viewers.
8 In the future, Chinese men will spend more on cosmetics in total than South Korean men.

C) Vocabulary in context Scan the text and find words that mean:

1 very important
2 per head
3 say in advance that something will happen
4 quickly growing
5 often and repeatedly
6 word or phrase
7 people who watch TV
8 feeling good about yourself

D) Now you Do you think it is OK for men to use skin-care products and makeup? Why or why not? Talk to a partner.

I can understand and talk about men's interest in cosmetics.

Culture focus
The right clothes

A 〔33〕 **Rob Hall from the company Asia-Pacific Business Specialists is talking about the importance of the right clothes in the business world. Listen to his presentation and answer the questions.**

1 How should you dress if you don't know a company's dress code?
2 Why is business dress often casual in Indonesia?
3 Which clothes are not acceptable on "casual Friday"?
4 How has business dress in Japan changed, and why did this happen?
5 Why should women in Japan wear formal clothes for business?

B 〔33〕 **Listen again and check (✔) the correct answer.**

1 Men normally wear business suits in . . .

☐ **A** formal meetings in the Philippines.
☐ **B** banks in Australia.
☐ **C** most offices in Indonesia.

2 In which country should you wear your best socks?

☐ **A** Australia
☐ **B** Indonesia
☐ **C** Thailand

3 What should women avoid in Indonesia?

☐ **A** sleeveless blouses
☐ **B** pants suits
☐ **C** dresses

4 What should a businessman wear on his first visit to Jakarta?

☐ **A** a long-sleeved batik shirt
☐ **B** a jacket and tie
☐ **C** a formal suit

5 Which two countries have "casual Friday"?

☐ **A** Australia and Japan
☐ **B** Australia and the Philippines
☐ **C** The Philippines and Japan

6 A foreigner who does business in the Philippines should wear . . .

☐ **A** a Barong Tagalog.
☐ **B** an open-necked shirt.
☐ **C** a long-sleeved shirt.

C **Now you** **What kinds of clothes do men and women in your country wear for:**

1 business meetings?
2 informal parties?
3 formal parties?
4 weddings and similar ceremonies?
5 leisure time?

Barong Tagalog

I can *understand how to dress for business in Asia-Pacific.*

The world of work

1 Business situation
Different types of work

A) Work with a partner. What jobs can you see in the pictures? Which job would you most like to do and which would you least like to do? Give reasons.

B) [34] Listen to Ethan Thomas interviewing Florence Wu and Sam Kao. List the jobs that you hear. Put them into two groups depending on the kind of training you need for each job:

Academic training: . . .   Vocational training: . . .

C) [34] Listen again and check (✔) the reasons Florence gives for the increasing interest in vocational training.

1 Many people think that a vocational skill is more useful in the job market. ☐
2 More and more people with academic training can't find jobs anymore. ☐
3 More people believe that they can be happy in a non-academic job. ☐
4 The image of vocational training has improved. ☐
5 Studying is no longer important. ☐

D) Now answer the questions.

1 What is the definition of success for many Asians?
2 What was the reason Sam changed his job?
3 Can you describe Sam's old job.
4 How is his new job different?
5 How did Sam's parents react to his decision?
6 Why does Florence think the increased interest in vocational training is a good development?

....

▷ ▪ vocational training ▪ skill ▪ skilled
    ▪ unskilled ▪ status

I can understand a radio interview about different types of work.

A Look at Sam's statements from 1A, answer the questions and underline the correct words to complete the rule.

"If I **had wanted** to earn money, I **would have started** work at 18."
1 Did Sam want to earn money?   2 Did he start work at 18?

"I **wouldn't have changed** my job if I **had been** happy."
3 Did Sam change his job?   4 Was he happy?

> We use the third conditional to talk about things in the past that could have been different.
>
> We use *if* + **past simple / past perfect** and *would(n't) have* + **past participle / past perfect** in the main clause.

B Complete the sentences with the verbs in brackets.

1 If Tri *had wanted* (want) a different job, he would have gone to college.
2 I *wouldn't have found* (not find) a job if I hadn't done some vocational training.
3 Shota .... (not take) an unskilled job if he had found a job in his field.
4 So many people wouldn't have left the region if there .... (be) more jobs.
5 We .... (not manage) our work last week if we .... (not do) overtime.
6 I .... (be) happier with my last job if I .... (have) fixed hours.
7 If Ria .... (not find) a job when she left college last year, she .... (retrain).

C Say how things could have been different in Sam's life. Complete the sentence.

1 His parents wanted him to study so he went to college. If his parents *hadn't wanted him to study*, he wouldn't have gone to college.
2 He didn't start work at 18, so he didn't earn any money. If he ...., he would have earned some money.
3 At college he was good at math, so he became an engineer. If he hadn't been good at math, he ....
4 He wasn't happy because his job was so stressful. If his job ...., he would have been happy.
5 He wanted to earn more money, so he changed his job. If he ...., he wouldn't have changed his job.
6 He went to work in a car repair shop where he met his wife Lin. If he hadn't gone to work in the car repair shop, he ....

Sam's wife Lin

D Work with a partner. Say what could have been different.

1 I didn't study hard and I failed my math exam. *If I had studied harder, I would have passed it.*
2 I woke up late this morning and I missed the bus. *If I hadn't woken up late, . . .*
3 I didn't have enough money, so I didn't go on vacation.
4 I lent Harry $500 because he was in trouble.
5 I learned Chinese and went to work in Shanghai.

E **Now you** Tell your partner three things you did or didn't do and what happened.

▷ ▪ field ▪ overtime
  ▪ to retrain

> *I can* understand and use the third conditional.

Grammar focus
Focus 2: *Used to do*

F Look at the sentences from 1A and complete the rule.

I **used to** take work home.
I **didn't use to** look forward to work.
Did you **use to** worry a lot about your work?

> *Used to* + verb tells us that something was true or happened regularly in the ...., but is not true or doesn't happen now. The negative form is .... *to*, and the question form is .... *you* .... *to*?

G |35| Listen to the recording. Do you hear *used to* or *use to*? Check (✔) the correct answer.

1 ☐ used to	✔ use to		**4** ☐ used to	☐ use to
2 ☐ used to	☐ use to		**5** ☐ used to	☐ use to
3 ☐ used to	☐ use to		**6** ☐ used to	☐ use to

> **!**
> We use *used to* only to talk about the past.
> There is no present form of *used to*.

H Make sentences with *used to* (✔) or *didn't use to* (✘). Compare your sentences with a partner.

1 Computers (✔) be much bigger than they are today.
  Computers used to be much bigger than they are today.
2 Ji-yun (✘) drink tea, but now it's her favorite drink.
  Ji-yun didn't use to drink tea. Now it's her favorite drink.
3 Ahmed (✘) study hard, but now he wants to pass his exams.
4 Lin (✔) play the guitar, but she's out of practice.
5 Women (✘) work as much outside the home as they do today.
6 I (✔) go to parties, but now I prefer to stay at home.
7 People (✘) travel as much as they do now.
8 Our company (✔) employ more staff.

Computers used to be much bigger.

I Work in small groups.

A Find somebody who . . .
1 used to have a *tamagotchi*. *Did you use to . . . ?*
2 used to live in another town. (Where?)
3 used to have a favorite game. (Which?)
4 used to play a musical instrument. (What?)
  Find out why they don't do it anymore.

B Find somebody who . . .
5 didn't use to eat fast food, but does now.
6 didn't use to wear sneakers, but does now.
7 didn't use to like sports, but does now.
8 didn't use to study hard, but does now.
  Find out why they changed.

> *I can* ask and talk about the past, using used to do.

3 Listening and speaking
Working conditions and company benefits

A Match the company benefits 1 to 8 with the definitions A to H.

1 annual paid leave ....
2 maternity leave ....
3 paternity leave ....
4 pension plan ....
5 sick leave ....
6 unpaid leave ....
7 bonus ....
8 flextime ....

A time off work for the father of a new baby
B an additional payment
C number of days off work per year with full pay
D time off work with no pay
E time off to have a baby
F a fund for workers in their old age
G a system that allows you to choose when you start and finish work
H time off work because of illness

B [36] Listen to Alisa Boonliang talking about the working conditions and benefits in her company. Which of the benefits in 3A do you NOT hear?

C [36] Listen again. There are eight mistakes in the summary. Underline them, then correct them.

Alisa is an electrician and she has worked in an electronics company near London for seven years. It's not a very secure job, but the salary is excellent. She is paid for overtime and she gets a bonus twice a year. She gets five weeks annual paid leave. She doesn't get sick leave, but when she had a baby two years ago, she took fully paid maternity leave before her baby was born.
She has a regular nine-to-five job, so she can organize her work to fit her family life. She got a month's unpaid leave when her husband went abroad on vacation. When she is old, she'll have two pensions, one from the state and one from her company.

D Talking about ... work and jobs

Step 1: With your partner, take turns to ask and answer the questions.
1 What sort of job would you like to do?
2 What sort of daily work routine would you like to have (nine-to-five, flextime, part-time)? Why?
3 What should your job involve? What should it not involve? (Travel, teamwork, dealing with people, ...)

I want my job to involve a lot of traveling because I want to see the world.
I don't want ...

Step 2: Rank the benefits in 3A that are important to you (1 is the most important and 7 is the least important). Make a note of your reasons.

Step 3: Compare your ranking with a partner.

Flextime is very important to me because ...

▷ ▪ on leave ▪ nine-to-five job
▪ flextime

"Let me explain something about flextime. You still have to show up for work once in a while."

I can understand and talk about working conditions and company benefits.

Vocabulary focus
Work

A Find the pairs of opposites. There is one word/phrase you don't need.

at work	day shift	fixed hours	flextime	full-time	get fired
in work	night shift	*off work*	out of work	part-time	permanent
quit	skilled	tax	temporary	unskilled	

B Find words in 4A to match the definitions.

1 money from your wage or salary you
  have to pay to the government ....
2 leave your job ....
3 unemployed ....
4 employed ....
5 hours worked at night ....
6 lasting for a limited time ....
7 lose a job ....

YOU'RE FIRED!

C What kind of work would be best for each of these people?

a nine-to-five job   a part-time job   shift work   a job with flextime
a job with paid overtime   a temporary job

1

Ji-na wants to work during her college vacation.

2

Bom wants to earn some extra money in addition to his wage.

3

Nur needs to be flexible because of her family.

4

Shun wants a job with fixed hours.

5

Ting only wants to work in the mornings.

6

Joe wants to work in a factory where work goes on 24/7.

D Find the sentences A to H that have a meaning similar to sentences 1 to 8.

1 What do you do for a living? ....
2 Is it a very demanding job? ....
3 Is it a manual job? ....
4 Do you work for yourself? ....
5 How much do you make? ....
6 What does the job involve? ....
7 Did you need special training? ....
8 Why were you off work? ....

A Are you self-employed?
B What do you have to do?
C Is it a skilled job?
D Were you on vacation or sick leave?
E Do you work with your hands?
F What's your job?
G What's your salary?
H Is it hard work?

E Which is the odd word out?

1	**earn**	☐ a salary	☐ a wage	☒ tax
2	**team**	☐ player	☐ job	☐ work
3	**take**	☐ success	☐ work home	☐ annual leave
4	**vocational**	☐ employment	☐ training	☐ skill
5	**work**	☐ shifts	☐ a job	☐ overtime
6	**deal with**	☐ problems	☐ customers	☐ experience
7	**day**	☐ hours	☐ job	☐ shift
8	**lose**	☐ status	☐ your job	☐ flextime

F Idioms are often used in work and business. Choose the correct meaning of these idioms.

1	snowed under	☐ working in bad conditions	☐ very busy
2	dead-end	☐ time when a task must be finished	☐ without future prospects
3	up-and-coming	☐ becoming more and more successful	☐ getting famous
4	on paper	☐ in newspapers and magazines	☐ in theory
5	get out of a rut	☐ escape from a boring situation	☐ get promoted
6	off the record	☐ unemployed	☐ unofficial
7	talk shop	☐ talk about work	☐ discuss shopping
8	behind the scenes	☐ unseen	☐ top secret

G Use the idioms in 4F to complete the sentences.

1 The plan looks good ...., but will it work?
2 I'm completely .... I have so much to do.
3 Please don't .... while we're having lunch.
4 I changed my job because I wanted to ....
5 A lot of preparation went on .... before the trade show.
6 He's a very .... young man and will probably be a CEO one day.

H ▷ **Key words** Look at the words at the bottom of pages 63–66. Choose the best word to complete the sentences.

1 Selling fried chicken is a(n) .... job.
2 Shun couldn't find a job in his ...., so he .... and became a plumber.
3 We have ...., so we don't work fixed hours.
4 I won't be in the office next week. I'll be ....
5 How high is your .... in the organization?
6 A lot of young people prefer .... to college.
7 The ability to work as part of a team is a useful ....
8 Sam did a lot of .... and wasn't paid for it.

I can talk about different ways of working.

Reading

Tanshinfunin – living apart from the family

A) Before you read Look at the picture. Describe what you can see. Why do you think the man is taking the train? Tell a partner your ideas.

Asian Business **Online**

looks at *tanshinfunin* in Japan.

When his company asked Takumi Fukuda to move to Tokyo, his family had just bought a home on the northern coast as they wanted their children to have fresh air and space to play. So Mr. Fukuda and his wife agreed that he should go to his new job in the capital without the family. That was two years ago and he is still living in Tokyo alone.

The experience of Mr. Fukuda is not unusual in Japan. Fathers who are transferred to another city or country sometimes go alone and leave their families behind. These men are often jokingly called "bachelor husbands." There are many thousands of them in Japan and *tanshinfunin* has become a common household word.

There are a number of reasons for this situation: the first has to do with land prices, which are extremely high in Japan. Once you have a house or an apartment, you don't give it up easily. Another reason has to do with the children's schooling. The Japanese education system is very demanding. It is not easy to get into a good high school or university, so parents are unwilling to interrupt their kids' education. There may also be elderly parents to look after at home. So rather than uproot the family, the father commutes by plane or *shinkansen* (bullet train), usually returning home once or twice a month.

In Japan it is normal for employees to make sacrifices for their companies, and companies move people around much more than in other countries without stopping to ask "Is it convenient for you to be transferred now?" His private responsibilities are the employee's problem, not the company's. "I get lonely and I miss my family a lot," says Mr. Fukuda, "but I know the separation will only last a few years, and it will certainly have a positive effect on my career."

B) Scanning for detail Read the article and complete the sentences.

1 Takumi Fukuda and his family had just bought a house on the northern coast when . . .
2 Mr. Fukuda has been living in Tokyo . . .
3 *Tanshinfunin* has become a common household word because . . .
4 High land prices in Japan mean that people don't . . .
5 People are unwilling to interrupt their kids' education because . . .
6 Apart from high land prices and children's education, another reason for *tanshinfunin* is that . . .
7 Employees in Japan accept the fact that their company moves them around because . . .
8 Mr. Fukuda has accepted his situation because . . .

C) Meaning in context Find these words in the article. Can you guess their meaning? How did you guess?

| transferred | bachelor | elderly | uproot | sacrifice | convenient |

D) Now you What do think of *tanshinfunin* as a way of life? Would you ever live like this?

I can understand an article about employees living away from home.

A Lisa Lai has applied for a job. Look at the cover letter she sent with her résumé and number the parts.

1 other skills
2 details of experience
3 final comments
4 address of the company and name of the contact person
5 her qualifications
6 reference to enclosures
7 where she saw the advertisement

Newton Nanosystems
Attn. Mr. David Croft
231 Ventura Blvd. ☐
Los Angeles, CA 91356
United States

Dear Mr. Croft:

I saw your advertisement for a systems administrator on the website of *The Straits Times*.
I would like to apply for this position. ☐

After completing my education at the Raffles Commercial College, Singapore, I did a three-year internship with the company Nether Software, a small but successful company with 12 employees. ☐ Since 2015 I have worked at Software Solutions Ltd. in Singapore as a junior systems administrator. I not only have experience with software systems but also in running an office with a staff of 20. ☐

I speak and write English fluently. I also speak Mandarin, which would be useful, as I see from your website that you do business with China. ☐

I enclose my résumé and copies of my certificates. I would be pleased to provide references if required. ☐

I would welcome the opportunity to work in an international company in the United States, and I believe I would be an excellent member of your staff. I hope you will consider my application, and I look forward to hearing from you soon. ☐

Sincerely,
Lisa Lai

B Read the advertisement. Write a cover letter to send with your application. Use 6A as a model.

Keen International Consultants Inc.

We are a dynamic company providing business services to corporate clients worldwide. We have a number of vacancies in our head office in Chicago for secretaries with good communication and computer skills and at least one foreign language.

Send your application and résumé to Ms. Cathy Watts at

Keen International Consultants Inc. 210 Norman St. #301, Chicago, IL 60642, United States
Phone: +1 312-943-8600 Fax: +1 312-943-8601

I can understand and write a cover letter.

TOEIC® practice

1 Listening

A 🔊 37 **Photographs** Listen, then choose the sentence that best describes the photograph.

1 A ☐   B ☐   C ☐   D ☐   2 A ☐   B ☐   C ☐   D ☐

B 🔊 38 **Question-Response** Listen carefully. Choose the best response to the sentence you hear.

Example: Has the letter arrived yet?

   A ✔ Yes, It's on your desk.
   B ☐ Yes, the ladder's outside.
   C ☐ Yes, I'll post it later.

1 A ☐   B ☐   C ☐   3 A ☐   B ☐   C ☐
2 A ☐   B ☐   C ☐   4 A ☐   B ☐   C ☐

2 Speaking

A **Describe a picture** Choose one of the pictures in 1A. Look at it for 30 seconds, then describe it in your own words.

B 🔊 39 **Propose a solution** You will hear a problem. Respond to the problem as if you work in a designer boutique. You have 30 seconds to think about a solution. Then you will have 60 seconds to speak. Show that you recognize the problem and propose a way of dealing with it.

> Hello, this is Kate Wilson. I'm a regular customer in your boutique, and so far I've been pretty satisfied with the stuff I've had from you. But two weeks ago, I bought a very expensive wool dress. I washed it yesterday and of course I followed the instructions on the label. But now it's shrunk. It's so small that I can't wear it. I'm just so disappointed. I didn't expect that from such an expensive item. I'm afraid I don't have the receipt anymore, but I paid for it with my credit card, so it will be on my statement at the end of the month.

3 Reading

Incomplete sentences Choose the best word to complete each sentence.

1 What would you have studied if you
   .... to college?
   - [ ] **A** go
   - [ ] **B** will go
   - [ ] **C** had gone
   - [ ] **D** went

2 .... to work for Toyota?
   - [ ] **A** Did you use
   - [ ] **B** Do you use
   - [ ] **C** Did you used
   - [ ] **D** Used you

3 What do you do for a ....
   - [ ] **A** job?
   - [ ] **B** living?
   - [ ] **C** work?
   - [ ] **D** wages?

4 Sam is happy .... his new job.
   - [ ] **A** by
   - [ ] **B** for
   - [ ] **C** on
   - [ ] **D** in

5 I'd like to .... for the job.
   - [ ] **A** work
   - [ ] **B** apply
   - [ ] **C** employ
   - [ ] **D** quit

6 Takumi doesn't mind ....
   - [ ] **A** to commute.
   - [ ] **B** that he commutes.
   - [ ] **C** commute.
   - [ ] **D** commuting.

4 Writing

Respond to a written request Reply to the email. Ask for at least TWO more pieces of information.

From: Dave Low
To: Bernie Stanbridge
Subject: Golf 2.0 Sportline red metallic

Hello Bernie,

Glad to hear you are interested in buying the car I advertised on the Auto Exchange website. To answer your questions: the car has had only one previous owner, and yes, I am prepared to go down on the advertised price of $10,000. You can come and see the car and take a test drive.

Please let me know if you need any more information.

Best wishes,
Dave

Business and the environment

1 Business situation
How green is your office?

A 🔊40 Jessica Asedillo is talking to her friend Lester about making her office more environmentally friendly. Listen to their conversation and check (✔) the correct answer.

1 Who had the idea of a new dress code?
- ☐ **A** Lester
- ☐ **B** Felix
- ☐ **C** Jessica

2 What shocked Felix?
- ☐ **A** the company's carbon footprint
- ☐ **B** his own carbon footprint
- ☐ **C** a commuter's carbon footprint

3 Lester always leaves his machines . . .
- ☐ **A** switched on.
- ☐ **B** switched off.
- ☐ **C** on standby.

4 What has Jessica's company banned?
- ☐ **A** water coolers
- ☐ **B** plastic cups
- ☐ **C** print-outs

5 Lester expects that in the future people will . . .
- ☐ **A** continue to use a lot of paper.
- ☐ **B** work in paperless offices.
- ☐ **C** not trust their computers.

6 Which statement about Lester is correct?
- ☐ **A** He doesn't believe in carbon footprints.
- ☐ **B** He is not interested in his carbon footprint.
- ☐ **C** He will check out his carbon footprint.

B 🔊40 Listen again and answer the questions.

1 What is the new office dress code in Jessica's company?
2 What is the reason for the new dress code?
3 What does Lester do to reduce his energy bills?
4 What did Felix tell Jessica about the CO_2 produced by commuters?
5 What reason does Lester give why we print out so many documents?

▷ ▪ carbon footprint ▪ environmentally friendly
  ▪ CO_2 ▪ to ban ▪ to recycle

I can understand a conversation about an environmentally friendly office.

Grammar focus

Focus 1: Reporting verbs and indirect questions

A) Read the transcript for the conversation in 1A on page 112. Find the sentences where these statements are reported and complete the rule.

"We will switch to a green cleaning company as soon as possible."
"One day we will have paperless offices."

In reported speech we change *will* to ....

B) Report what was said using the reporting verbs and *if* or *that*. Use each verb only once.

announced	~~asked~~	explained	promised	tell	wanted to know

1 "Will you help me figure out my carbon footprint?" Lester said to Jessica.
  Lester asked Jessica if she would help him figure out his carbon footprint.
2 "CO₂ is harmful to the environment," Jessica told Lester.
3 "I can make the office more environmentally friendly," Felix said to the CEO.
4 "I'll go to work by bus in the future," Lester told Jessica.
5 "Plastic cups will be banned," Felix told the staff.
6 "Do airplanes produce more CO_2 than other means of transportation?" Jessica said.

C) Read the transcript again and complete the indirect questions.

Direct questions with a question word	Indirect questions
1 How much CO_2 do commuters produce?	Do you know ....?
2 Why do you print out so many documents?	Felix asked us ....
3 How much less energy do they consume?	Have you any idea ....?

D) Say the questions again. Start with the expression in brackets.

1 How many aluminum cans do people throw away every year? (Do you know . . . ?)
  Do you know how many aluminum cans people throw away every year?
2 Where are the Greenpeace headquarters? (Jessica asked Felix . . .)
  Jessica asked Felix where the Greenpeace headquarters were.
3 How much CO_2 does a flight from Bangkok to Jakarta produce? (Do you have any idea . . . ?)
4 How much of the world's waste does the U.S. produce? (Can you tell me . . .)
5 In which countries are plastic shopping bags not allowed? (Jessica wanted to know . . .)
6 How much garbage does the average Australian family throw away every year? (Jessica asked Lester . . .)
7 Why is it important that we reduce pollution? (Can you explain . . .)
8 Which site did you use to get that information? (Do you remember . . . ?)

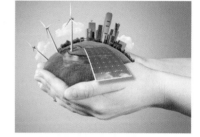

E) Now you Look on the Internet and find the answers to questions 1 to 6 in 2D. Compare your answers with a partner.

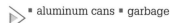

▷ ▪ aluminum cans ▪ garbage

I can report sentences about the future and use indirect questions.

Grammar focus
Focus 2: Review of conditionals

F Look at these conditional sentences from 1A and complete the chart.

1 I wouldn't have known that if Felix hadn't told me.
2 If we don't all become more environmentally friendly, we'll destroy the planet.
3 My energy bills would be much higher if I left everything on standby.

	Example sentence	*If* clause	Main clause
First conditional	2		*will* + infinitive
Second conditional			
Third conditional		past perfect	*would have* + . . .

G Match the two parts of the sentences.

1 If we drove hybrid cars, ...
2 If we took our own shopping bags to the supermarket, ...
3 If we hadn't gone on vacation by plane, ...
4 If we produced more renewable energy, ...
5 If we increase room temperature to 25 degrees, ...
6 If we hadn't left our machines on standby, ...
7 If we buy new energy-saving equipment,
8 If we continue to pollute our planet, ...

A our energy bills would have been lower.
B we'll destroy it.
C we would have helped reduce pollution.
D we would use less fuel.
E we wouldn't need so much coal, oil, and gas.
F we'll keep cooling costs down.
G we'll reduce our energy bills.
H we wouldn't need to use plastic ones.

H Put the verbs into the correct form.

1 If you take public transportation, you .... (help) to reduce pollution.
2 If we had gone by subway, we .... (avoid) the traffic jams.
3 If we .... (not change) our habits, pollution will get worse.
4 Companies .... (not transport) goods so far if people bought more local products.
5 If air pollution gets worse, we .... (not be) able to breathe.
6 It .... (be) better if you had taken your bottles to the recycling bin.
7 People .... (use) fewer plastic bags if they had to pay for them.

I Complete the sentences about yourself. Tell a partner.

1 I'll be happy if ....
2 I'd be really annoyed if ....
3 I wouldn't have come to school today if ....
4 If I have time on the weekend, I ....
5 If English wasn't so important, I ....
6 If you had forgotten my birthday, I ....

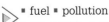

▷ ▪ fuel ▪ pollution
▪ renewable ▪ energy saving

I can use first, second, and third conditionals.

A Work with a partner. Make a list of the traditional ways of transporting goods. What are the advantages and disadvantages of each? Compare your lists with another pair.

Means of transportation	Advantages	Disadvantages
truck	• door-to-door service •	• pollution • ....

An unmanned drone

B 【41】 In a radio discussion program, Daniel Chan and Mike Anderson are talking about the future of business transportation. Listen and answer the questions.

1 What are the two main problems in business transportation today?
2 Why is transportation by ship cheaper than land transportation?
3 What is a major environmental concern about transportation by ship?
4 What innovation has a German company developed?
5 What innovation has a French company developed?
6 What are the advantages of drone transportation?

SkySails

C 【41】 Listen again. What do the numbers refer to?

| 10 to 15 | 82 | 90 | 150 | 8,000 |

D Talking about ... the environment

Step 1: Check (✔) the opinions you agree with.

1 Take-out coffee in throw-away cups should be banned.
2 There should be a high tax on bottled water.
3 Rich countries should pay more to fight global warming.
4 All countries should pay more to fight global warming.
5 Air travel should be more expensive.
6 We must replace nuclear power with alternative forms of energy.
7 Plastic shopping bags should cost money or be banned completely.
8 All cities should make drivers pay to drive into the city center.
9 We don't need hot water in public restrooms.
10 Commuting drivers should be paid to take passengers with them.

Step 2: Compare and discuss your opinions in small groups.

Step 3: In your groups make a list of dos and don'ts for saving energy. Compare your lists with another group and make a complete list of ideas for the whole class.

▷ ▪ freight ▪ carbon dioxide ▪ innovation
▪ wave energy ▪ contribution ▪ protection

I can discuss environmental issues.

4 Vocabulary focus
Focus 1: The environment

A Label the pictures with the correct words. Compare your answers with a partner.

| global warming | hybrid car | nuclear power plant | plastic bottles |
| recycling bins | solar power plant | water pollution | wind farm |

1 ....   2 ....   3 ....   4 ....

5 ....   6 ....   7 ....   8 ....

B Decide with a partner which of the things in 4A are good for the environment and which are bad. Give reasons for your answers.

C Replace the words in bold with words that have the same meaning (A–H). Then tell a partner which things you do or don't do.

1 **Go to and from work** by bus and not by car.	E	**A** recycle
2 **Don't use** cleaning fluids with lots of chemicals.	....	**B** switch
3 **Use** as many things as possible **again**.	....	**C** prevent
4 Don't **buy** products with a lot of packaging.	....	**D** research
5 **Change** from a laser printer to an inkjet printer.	....	**E** ~~commute~~
6 **Check out** your carbon footprint.	....	**F** conserve
7 **Save** water whenever possible.	....	**G** avoid
8 **Stop** further damage to the environment.	....	**H** purchase

D Work with a partner.

Student A: Go to Partner file 8.
Student B: Look at the picture on this page. Describe it to your partner.

Who can you see (number, male/female, appearance)?
Where are they?
What are they doing and why?
What else can you see (number, description of objects or people)?
Do you ever wear a mask? Why or why not?

I can talk about the environment.

E Match words 1 to 6 with the synonyms A to F. Then complete the sentences with the word pairs.

1 cautious	B	A put off
2 rich	....	B ~~careful~~
3 reliable	....	C furious
4 postponed	....	D polluted
5 mad	....	E wealthy
6 filthy	....	F dependable

Synonyms

1 **A:** I don't think people are *careful* enough when they use the Internet.
   B: I agree. We should all be more *cautious*.

2 **A:** May's family must be .... They have two houses and a yacht.
   B: Yes, I believe they are very ....

3 **A:** Was your boss .... when you told her what happened?
   B: She certainly was. I've never seen her so .... !

4 **A:** A lot of the rivers in my country are ....
   B: Yes, unfortunately some in my country are pretty .... too.

5 **A:** If Shun promises to do something, he'll do it. He's very ....
   B: Good. I need somebody .... to do the job.

6 **A:** Has the meeting been .... ?
   B: Yes, it's been .... until Friday.

Furious!

F Match words 1 to 6 with the opposites A to F. Then agree with the statements below.

1 dangerous	....	A economical
2 pessimistic	....	B challenging
3 dumb	....	C modern
4 wasteful	....	D safe
5 simple	....	E optimistic
6 ancient	....	F smart

We can agree with someone by using *not very* and the opposite:
A: *This exercise is easy, isn't it?*
B: *You're right. It's not very difficult.*

1 That bridge looks dangerous.
2 It's wasteful to use so much water.
3 That's a pessimistic view of the future.
4 Tri's question was really dumb.
5 I thought the tasks were rather simple.
6 Your computer looks pretty ancient.

You're right. It doesn't look very safe.
Absolutely. It's . . .
I agree. . . .

G ▷ **Key words** Look at the words at the bottom of pages 73–76. Choose the best words to complete the sentences.

1 Another word for "forbid" is ".................."
2 Save and recycle .... and plastic bottles.
3 CO_2 stands for ....
4 Lester discovered that he had a huge ....
5 We must all make a(n) .... toward protecting the environment.
6 In the future, ships will use solar power and ....
7 British English: rubbish, American English: ....
8 A(n) .... is a new idea or invention.

I can use synonyms and opposites.

A **Before you read** What kinds of transportation do you have in the cities in your country? Are they environmentally friendly?

Asian Business **Online**
looks at the future of a traditional means of transportation in Southeast Asia.

Tuk-tuks – sometimes called "auto rickshaws" – are a symbol of traditional life and a tourist attraction in many parts of Southeast Asia. Unfortunately, they are also a noisy, smelly, and dirty means of transportation.

In Bangkok, for example, about 70,000 gasoline-powered tuk-tuks drive around the city alongside four million cars and two-and-a-half million motorcycles, all producing carbon dioxide. And Bangkok is not the only Southeast Asian city with a serious pollution problem. But now inventors have come up with a greener vehicle – a solar-powered tuk-tuk.

"These tuk-tuks are quiet and produce zero CO_2," says inventor Narong Willapana. "They have a maximum speed of 60 kilometers an hour and can cover 120 kilometers on one charge."

The three-wheeled vehicles run on batteries charged by a solar roof panel. Gasoline is expensive, but solar-powered tuk-tuks cost next-to-nothing to run. However, they cost about $10,000 dollars to buy – about double the cost of a conventional vehicle. "I think they're a great idea and I would be happy to drive one," says Bangkok tuk-tuk driver Sawai Nantakarn, "but most of us would never be able to afford it unless the government helped us."

As more and more countries are looking for cleaner transportation options, interest in the new vehicles is spreading to other parts of Southeast Asia. An Australian company has already built a tuk-tuk factory in Cambodia to produce solar-powered vehicles, and a spokesperson says the company has begun discussions with Vietnam and the Philippines.

Perhaps some day soon you will no longer hear the "tuk-tuk" sound that is so familiar today in Southeast Asia.

B **Skim the article** What do the numbers refer to?

| 60 | 120 | 10,000 | 70,000 | 2.5 million |

C **Scanning for detail.** Read the text and find . . .

1 another name for a tuk-tuk.
2 three disadvantages of a conventional tuk-tuk.
3 three advantages of a solar-powered tuk-tuk.
4 one big disadvantage of the new green tuk-tuk.
5 which three Asian countries the Australian company is dealing with.

D **Vocabulary in context** Scan the text and find words that mean:

1 a person who finds something new
2 driven by energy from the sun
3 being part of a culture that is handed down
4 take in and store electricity
5 common, well known
6 choices
7 very, very little

I can understand an article about solar-powered transportation.

Culture focus
Culture quiz

Can you remember what you learned in Units 1 to 7 about different cultures? Try this quiz. There is one point for every correct answer.

Part 1 Name . . .

1 two countries where employees get the highest paid leave.
2 a country that Professor Leaver thinks has the hardest workers in the world.
3 two countries where people often do not take their annual leave because they are worried about their jobs.
4 two countries where a gift might be seen as a bribe.
5 a country where attractive gift wrapping is important.
6 two "high-context" cultures.

Part 2 Answer the questions.

7 Why did the Beijing Olympics begin on August 8, 2008?
8 Why is there no thirteenth floor in many New York skyscrapers?
9 Which color is associated with good luck and happiness in both the East and West?
10 Where should you give gifts in pairs and why?
11 Is conflict part of the business culture in a high-context or low-context culture?
12 What is "casual Friday"?

Part 3 What was the mistake and why did it happen?

13 A British company tried to sell a product in Japan at a price of ¥999,99. The product didn't sell well.
14 A Chinese businessman visited a company in Indonesia. After negotiations were completed, his hosts offered him a small gift and he refused it. The hosts were very upset.
15 A beverage company changed its vending machines from dark blue to light blue in Southeast Asia. Sales fell.
16 An Australian businesswoman went to South Korea to meet her business partners for the first time. They looked shocked when she asked them some direct questions about themselves.
17 A German businesswoman held negotiations with her Thai business partners. She was very surprised when they said they did not need their agreements in writing, but she insisted.
18 A British businessman visited his business partners in Japan. They exchanged gifts. The businessman opened his gift immediately and was surprised that his business partners didn't open theirs.
19 A Philippine businessman went to work for an Australian company, where they had "casual Friday." It was hot, so he turned up in his shorts.
20 A Thai businessman went to the Philippines for a formal business meeting. He wore a dark suit, white shirt, and tie. His business partners were wearing Barong Tagalog shirts and looked at their visitor in surprise.

Score
18–20 points: Very good
15–17 points: Good
13–14 points: OK
0–12 points: Read the *Culture focus* pages and the transcript in Units 1, 3, 5, and 7 again!

Finding a job

1 Business situation
Job hunting

A) 🔊42 **Sumalee Jainukal from Thailand and Umar Faizal from Malaysia are in their final year at an international college. They are looking at online job advertisements. Listen to their conversation and note the skills and qualities they each have. Write *S* for Sumalee, *U* for Umar, and *N* for skills which are NOT mentioned.**

ambitious	....	hardworking	....
enthusiastic	....	reliable	....
flexible	....	speaks foreign languages	....
good communication skills	....	team player	....
good with people	....		

B) 🔊42 **Listen to the conversation in 1A again. Are the statements true, false, or not stated? Correct the false statements.**

	True	False	Not stated
1 Fit-for-Fun is looking for a new team for their fitness center.	☐	☐	☐
2 All applicants for the Fit-for-Fun job will be interviewed.	☐	☐	☐
3 Sumalee has missed the closing date for applications.	☐	☐	☐
4 The salary for the marketing trainee is negotiable.	☐	☐	☐
5 The marketing job is suitable for career beginners.	☐	☐	☐
6 The training program lasts for three months.	☐	☐	☐
7 Umar is interested in a job in Kuala Lumpur.	☐	☐	☐
8 The construction company is looking for experienced staff.	☐	☐	☐
9 Umar works for a travel agency every summer.	☐	☐	☐

C) **Now you** **What kind of job will you look for when you graduate? Describe the kind of company you would like to work for. How will you look for a job?**

▷ ▪ to shortlist ▪ negotiable ▪ entry-level
▪ ambitious ▪ reference ▪ résumé

I can understand a conversation about job hunting.

A Read the statements from 1A and complete the answers to the questions.

1 Sumalee said: "I wish I had seen the ad before."
   Q: Did Sumalee see the ad before?
   A: No, she didn't, but she wishes she .... it before.
2 Umar said: "If only I hadn't said no."
   Q: Did Umar say no?
   A: Yes, he ...., but he wishes he .... no.

B Look at the tenses in 2A and complete the rule.

To express regret about past actions we use *wish* or *if only* with the .... tense.

C Look at the pictures and complete the sentences. Use the verbs given and add your own ending.

1	2	3
Ken	Yuka	Kasem

4	5	6
Nur	Ben	Ahmed

1 Ken / wish / pass   *Ken wishes he had passed his exam.*
   He thinks: "If only / study"   *"If only I had studied harder."*
2 Yuka / wish / not crash   ....
   She thinks: "If only / drive"   ....
3 Kasem / wish / not eat   ....
   He thinks: "If only / not be"   ....
4 Nur / wish / not lose   ....
   She thinks: "If only / take care" ....
5 Ben / wish / not go   ....
   He thinks: "If only / leave"   ....
6 Ahmed / wish / listen   ....
   He thinks: "If only / take advice" ....

D Work with a partner. Tell your partner three regrets you have about things you've done or haven't done. Think about:

| friends | family | college | money |

▷ ▪ to apply ▪ application
  ▪ applicant

I can express regret about events in the past.

E Can you remember the grammar from Units 1 to 10? Try this quiz. There is one point for every correct answer.

1 I wish I .... more leisure time.

- [ ] **A** would have
- [ ] **B** have
- [ ] **C** had

2 Should we get the documents .... ?

- [ ] **A** translated
- [ ] **B** translate
- [ ] **C** translating

3 Lisa only has .... customers.

- [ ] **A** a little
- [ ] **B** a bit
- [ ] **C** a few

4 Where .... your business cards printed?

- [ ] **A** have you
- [ ] **B** do you have
- [ ] **C** does it have

5 I stopped .... plastic bags a long time ago.

- [ ] **A** to use
- [ ] **B** using
- [ ] **C** the use

6 I'm looking forward .... our business partners.

- [ ] **A** to meeting
- [ ] **B** to meet
- [ ] **C** meeting

7 .... information you gave me was useful.

- [ ] **A** An
- [ ] **B** Many
- [ ] **C** The

8 Lin .... an email when her computer crashed.

- [ ] **A** wrote
- [ ] **B** was writing
- [ ] **C** will write

9 Ben .... getting ready, so I waited for him.

- [ ] **A** hadn't finished
- [ ] **B** didn't finish
- [ ] **C** wasn't finishing

10 My boss asked me .... the appointment.

- [ ] **A** that I not forget
- [ ] **B** to not forget
- [ ] **C** not to forget

11 My laptop is missing. I hope it ....

- [ ] **A** isn't being stolen.
- [ ] **B** hasn't been stolen.
- [ ] **C** can't be stolen.

12 If Isamu .... to college, he would have done vocational training.

- [ ] **A** didn't go
- [ ] **B** wouldn't have gone
- [ ] **C** hadn't gone

Score

11–12 points: Very good
9–10 points: Good
7–8 points: OK
0–6 points: Practice!

A Job seekers often do things wrong when they write their applications or go for an interview. Make a list of the mistakes job seekers make.

Make spelling mistakes on a job application, arrive late for an interview, . . .

B ⟨43⟩ Helen Chu is a freelance management trainer. Listen to her talking about the mistakes that job seekers make. Were any of the mistakes on your list?

C ⟨43⟩ Listen again and complete the sentences.

1 Part of Helen's work is to ....
2 A candidate turned up wearing ....
3 The telephone interview was interrupted because the woman ....
4 A cover letter should be .... and say something about what you can bring to the job. It shouldn't ....
5 Have somebody check your résumé for ....
6 Doing research before you go to an interview shows that you ....
7 It makes you look professional if you ....
8 Private pictures on social media pages should be ....
9 At the interview be .... and make .... with the interviewers.
10 If asked about your weaknesses, say .... and what you are doing ....

D **Talking about ...** job interviews

Step 1: Work in groups of four. Students A and B write a job advertisement together. Students C and D write a different job advertisement. You can look at some online job ads for ideas. The advertisement should include:

- what the company is offering: job description, working conditions, company benefits (see Unit 8).
- what applicants should offer: qualifications, skills, and personal qualities.
- the closing date for applications.
- where and to whom applications should be sent.

Step 2: With your partner think about what interview questions you will ask candidates. Ask about: qualifications, skills, strengths and weaknesses, hobbies, plans for the future, . . .

Step 3: Exchange your advertisements. Read the new ad carefully. Imagine you have applied for the job and have been invited to an interview. Think about what you will say and make notes.

Step 4: Students A and B interview Students C and D. Decide which of the two candidates is suitable for the job. Give reasons. Then change roles.

▷ ▪ management trainer ▪ strength
▪ weakness

I can take part in a job interview.

4 Vocabulary focus

Focus 1: Qualifications, skills, and personal qualities

A Make a chart and put the words into the correct columns. (Some words may go in two columns.)

ambitious	college degree	communicative	creative
driver's license	foreign languages	friendly	good leader
good listener	good with people	motivated
organizing abilities	patient	pleasant personality
school-leaving certificate	self-confident	specialist training
team player	university qualification	work experience

Qualifications	Skills	Personal qualities
college degree . . .	good leader . . .	ambitious . . .

B Work with a partner. Which skills, qualifications, and personal qualities do you need to do these jobs?

1 a nurse
2 a bus driver
3 a graphic designer
4 a plastic surgeon
5 an office assistant
6 a flight attendant
7 a car mechanic
8 a hotel receptionist
9 a web designer
10 an elementary school teacher

That's true. We did advertise for someone who "works well under pressure" . . .

C Which words go together? There may be more than one answer.

1 apply	E	**A** an applicant
2 write	....	**B** a job offer
3 interview	....	**C** an interview
4 answer	....	**D** your best
5 provide	....	**E** for a job
6 accept	....	**F** references
7 shortlist	....	**G** a receptionist
8 look	....	**H** an application
9 work as	....	**I** a résumé
10 negotiate	....	**J** a job advertisement
11 submit	....	**K** a salary
12 prepare for	....	**L** candidates

D ▷ **Key words** Look at the words at the bottom of pages 81–84. Choose the best words to complete the sentences.

1 The company received over 100 .... for the job they advertised.
2 Is the salary fixed or is it .... ?
3 My last employer gave me a very good ....
4 Isamu is .... and hopes to be CEO one day.
5 Lee got a .... to help him train for the interview.
6 I'm not sure if ambition is a(n) .... or a(n) ....
7 If a job is suitable for beginners, it is a(n) .... - .... position.
8 To .... means to make a list of the most suitable ....

I can talk about skills, qualifications, and personal qualities.

E Can you remember the vocabulary from Units 1 to 10? Try this quiz. There is one point for every correct answer.

Part 1 Complete the sentences with the correct word.

1 We must finish the report today if we want to meet the d...................
2 To find a good work-life balance you have to set p...................
3 A person who takes a franchise license is a f...................
4 The noun from "reliable" is r...................
5 To l................... a product means to put it on the market.
6 A t................... z................... is a region where the time is the same.
7 Nuri took the m................... of the last meeting.
8 Don't blame me! It's not my f...................

Part 2 Choose the correct answer.

9 A market researcher's job is to .... data.
  ☐ **A** gather
  ☐ **B** spend
  ☐ **C** arrange

10 I need colleagues that I can count ....
  ☐ **A** for.
  ☐ **B** on.
  ☐ **C** up.

11 .... are interesting.
  ☐ **A** The news
  ☐ **B** Economics
  ☐ **C** Her clothes

12 If you work with your hands, you do .... work.
  ☐ **A** academic
  ☐ **B** manual
  ☐ **C** unskilled

13 If you have too much to do, you are ....
  ☐ **A** snowed under.
  ☐ **B** in a rut.
  ☐ **C** up-and-coming.

14 The opposite of "dumb" is ....
  ☐ **A** silly.
  ☐ **B** noisy.
  ☐ **C** smart.

Part 3 Complete each sentence with key words from the box.

excursion	human resources	improvement
raw materials	recycling	target group

15 .... means using things again and again.
16 .... is the department responsible for hiring and training staff.
17 The people you want to sell your product to are your ....
18 You need .... to manufacture products.
19 A(n) .... is a short trip, for example a day out.
20 A(n) .... is a change to make things better.

Score
18–20 points: Very good
15–17 points: Good
12–14 points: OK
0–11 points: Practice!

Partner files

Partner file 1

Unit 2   2D

Student A: Ask your partner questions about the things you can see in your pictures. Answer his/her questions about their pictures. Ask three questions for each picture. Use *have* or *get something done*.

1 *Have you ever gotten / had …?*   **2** *How often do you …?*   **3** *When did you last …?*

A wash – car   **B** take – photograph   **C** check – eyes   **D** make – key

Partner file 2

Unit 2   3C

Student A: Look at the information below. Student B will ask you some questions.

Subway

If you're hungry, it's the easiest thing to get a delicious sandwich made at Subway. At any Subway restaurant, you can have your favorite sandwich made. The person who makes your sandwich is called a "sandwich artist." Your sandwich will be made with fresh bread and healthy ingredients.

The company was founded in the United States in 1965. Now, Subway has more than 40,000 global locations. All new franchise owners have to attend a Subway training course. The time is spent in the classroom and on-site at a Subway franchise. They take an exam at the end of the course. If they pass the exam, they can apply to open a Subway restaurant.

Now ask Student B questions and fill in the missing information.

United Parcel Service

With the help of UPS, you can (*do what?*) .... at any time. The company was founded (*when?*) .... It was a time when more and more businesses and private individuals needed to (*do what?*) .... UPS founder, (*name?*) ...., saw a business opportunity, so he borrowed $100 (*why?*) .... Most deliveries were made (*how?*) .... Today UPS delivers (*how many?*) .... packages and documents a day (*how?*) .... One important condition for new UPS franchise owners is that (*what?*) .... and have to pass an exam to prove it.

Partner file 3

Unit 5   3E

Student A

A Lion airplane with 120 passengers and crew on board hit a cow and skidded off the landing strip after it had landed at Jalaluddin Airport on Sulawesi, Indonesia, early yesterday morning. The pilot said that as he was landing he saw three animals on the runway and thought they were dogs. The cows had escaped from a nearby field and had wandered onto the runway. Some of the passengers had to leave through the emergency doors. No one was injured, but one of the cows was killed. The airport was closed for several hours, which affected people's travel plans for the Eid holiday.

Partner file 4

Unit 5   3E

Student B

In the Philippines, one of Asia's fastest growing economies, imports of raw materials have increased to their highest level in three years. Large quantities of metals and chemicals are needed for rebuilding after the damage caused by natural disasters in recent years. But raw materials are also needed to meet growing demand for the country's key exports, such as electronics and clothes. Imports in January hit $1.4 billion, up 21.8 percent compared with January last year. China was the biggest source of imports to the Philippines, with the United States in second place. "Increased imports now mean increased exports later," said a government spokesperson.

Partner file 5

Unit 5 4H

Student A: You live and work in Kuala Lumpur in Malaysia. It is a seven-hour flight to Tokyo and you hate flying. Apart from the time spent on the trip itself, you think a lot of time is wasted in face-to-face meetings. You prefer videoconferencing because you can do it from your own office; it saves time and money, and you don't have to socialize with the other participants afterwards. You have never worked with digital workspace before, but it sounds like a good idea and you would like to try it.

Listen to the others' opinions and give yours. Use some of the phrases from 4F.

Partner file 6

Unit 5 4H

Student B: You live and work in Manila in the Philippines. You enjoy flying and don't mind traveling to regular team meetings. Emailing and telephoning are useful, and you have worked with digital workspace before. They are all practical communication tools, but you think face-to-face communication is important in order to get to know your co-workers well. You don't think Skyping or videoconferencing are a good idea because technology is sometimes unreliable.

Listen to the others' opinions and give yours. Use some of the phrases from 4F.

Partner file 7

Unit 5 4H

Student C: You live and work in Jakarta in Indonesia. You are enthusiastic about any form of technological communication. You also think that face-to-face contact in regular meetings is a good idea, but not every month. You think that every two months would be enough as traveling takes a lot of time. You believe that each member of the team should take a turn to host the meetings in his/her own country.

Listen to the others' opinions and give yours. Use some of the phrases from 4F.

Partner file 8

Unit 9 4D

Student A: Look at the picture. Describe it to your partner.

Who can you see (number, male/female, appearance)?
Where are they?
What are they doing and why?
What else can you see (number, description of objects or people)?
What do you think has happened?

Irregular verbs

Infinitive	Past simple	Past participle ("3rd form")
be	was/were	been
beat	beat	beaten
become	became	become
begin	began	begun
bite	bit	bitten
break	broke	broken
bring	brought	brought
build	built	built
buy	bought	bought
catch	caught	caught
choose	chose	chosen
come	came	come
cost	cost	cost
cut	cut	cut
do	did	done
draw	drew	drawn
drink	drank	drunk
drive	drove	driven
eat	ate	eaten
fall	fell	fallen
feel	felt	felt
find	found	found
fly	flew	flown
forget	forgot	forgotten
get	got	got/gotten
give	gave	given
go	went	gone
grow	grew	grown
have	had	had
hear	heard	heard
hit	hit	hit
hold	held	held
hurt	hurt	hurt
keep	kept	kept
know	knew	known

Infinitive	Past simple	Past participle ("3rd form")
lead	led	led
leave	left	left
lend	lent	lent
lose	lost	lost
make	made	made
mean	meant	meant
meet	met	met
put	put	put
read	read	read
ride	rode	ridden
rise	rose	risen
run	ran	run
say	said	said
see	saw	seen
sell	sold	sold
send	sent	sent
set	set	set
show	showed	shown/showed
sit	sat	sat
sleep	slept	slept
speak	spoke	spoken
spend	spent	spent
stand	stood	stood
steal	stole	stolen
swim	swam	swum
take	took	taken
teach	taught	taught
tell	told	told
think	thought	thought
throw	threw	thrown
understand	understood	understood
wake	woke	woken
wear	wore	worn
win	won	won
write	wrote	written

Transcripts

Unit 1

Track 1

Ji-yun: Hi, Ted, Hi, Scott. How are things? Are you looking forward to the weekend?

Ted: Sure am. What about you, Scott?

Scott: Not me. I'm way behind schedule on my project, so I guess I'll have to put in extra time on the weekend to meet the deadline.

Ji-yun: Oh, not again, Scott! You put in extra time nearly every weekend. That can't be good for you.

Scott: I know. I wish I had more free time, and I wish I didn't get so stressed out. It's difficult to organize my time. Ted, you're good at time management. How do you do it?

Ted: Well, for a start I keep all my appointments in my iCal agenda, and I make to-do lists and decide on my priorities.

Scott: Oh, to-do lists are a waste of time. Things always come up that you didn't plan for.

Ted: Right, that's why it's important to be flexible, but lists are useful so you don't forget anything.

Ji-yun: Ted's right. It's helpful to make a daily list, so you can keep track of all the things you have to do.

Scott: Yeah, I suppose you're right. I wish I was better organized. I seem to waste a lot of time on unimportant tasks. I always think it's good to do them first, you know, sort of get them out of the way before I start on the big tasks.

Ji-yun: But it's *not* good to miss your deadlines.

Scott: I know. I wish someone could show me how to manage my time better.

Ted: Look, Scott, I'd be happy to show you how iCal works, but of course it's necessary to keep your lists up-to-date and to set priorities. The computer program will help you to keep on schedule, but it won't do your work for you!

Ji-yun: And I have a book I can lend you about improving your quality of life. It's full of tips about managing your time better and avoiding stress.

Scott: Thanks, Ji-yun. I just wish there were more hours in a day. My boss always tells me "Time is money," but I never seem to have enough time – or enough money!

Track 2

Interviewer: Welcome to our program. Our topic today is work-life balance. Work-life balance means finding the right balance between work hours and leisure time. Our guest today is businessman Takumi Ito. Takumi, you had a problem. Can you tell us about it?

Takumi: Yes, I have a home decorating company in Yokohama. My problem was that most of our business is done on the web, so in a twelve-hour workday, I spent about ten hours a day at the computer or on my phone. I began to feel like a robot.

Interviewer: But your business was very successful, wasn't it?

Takumi: Well, I was making a lot of money, but I wasn't happy. I felt as if my life was dominated by technology, and I woke up one day and thought: I wish I could escape from the digital world for at least a few hours a week.

Interviewer:	So what was the solution you came up with?
Takumi:	I decided to create an "escape room" in my company's headquarters.
Interviewer:	What do you mean exactly?
Takumi:	It's a room where there's no computer monitor, no Internet connection, no Wi-Fi, no TV – a room to escape to.
Interviewer:	How much time do you spend there?
Takumi:	It's difficult to say exactly. It depends on my schedule, but I'd say between three to five hours a week on average. I wish I could spend more time there.
Interviewer:	How's the room furnished?
Takumi:	Very simply. I have a couple of sofas, a coffee table, and a small table for a coffee machine and an old FM radio.
Interviewer:	What do you do in your escape room?
Takumi:	I read or listen to music on the radio. Somehow I can think more clearly there, and I become more creative. But sometimes I don't think at all. I just lie back and relax.
Interviewer:	Do you always spend time there alone?
Takumi:	Mostly, but sometimes friends or co-workers drop by – without their cell phones, of course!
Interviewer:	What do they think of your escape room?
Takumi:	At first they thought it was a weird idea, but now they can see that the room is good for me. My time-out makes me better balanced, and I can manage stress much better than I did before.
Interviewer:	Takumi, thank you for the interview.
Takumi:	My pleasure.

Track 3

Linda:	Professor Leaver, about 40 percent of Australians say they work too hard. Does your research confirm this?
Prof. Leaver:	Yes, it does. Our study found that Australians work very hard – despite their reputation for being relaxed and laid back. They work long hours, are very stressed, and have a poor work-life balance.
Linda:	How many hours a week do they work on average?
Prof. Leaver:	The average workweek is now 40 hours, and one in five people works more than 50 hours a week.
Linda:	South Korea and Japan have a reputation for hard work. What did your research show?
Prof. Leaver:	In Japan things are changing. The salaryman who went to his office at 9 AM and finished his workday at 2 AM in a bar with his colleagues is not as common as a few years ago. Many younger employees are looking for a better work-life balance. The average work time in Japan is now the same as in Australia.
Linda:	And in South Korea?
Prof. Leaver:	The Koreans seem to be the hardest-working people in the world. Working hard is part of their culture. On average, they work 45 hours a week. In addition, there may be a two-hour commute to work and the same to return home.
Linda:	In which other countries do the workers put in long hours?
Prof. Leaver:	Statistics show that the average number of work hours in some South American countries such as Argentina and Chile is over 40 per week. It's the same in some Eastern European countries, such as Poland and Hungary.
Linda:	But working longer doesn't mean working better, does it?
Prof. Leaver:	No, it doesn't. German workers, for example, work an average of 36 hours a

week, yet Germany has a very high level of productivity.

Linda: What about annual leave?

Prof. Leaver: When it comes to paid leave, European countries lead the world in giving paid leave to their workers. Portugal and Austria offer the most days off – an average of 35 days per year including paid public holidays. Australians have a legal right to four weeks paid annual leave. In Japan the legal minimum is 10 days, and in South Korea it is 15. But many people in these countries do not take all the leave they are allowed as they are worried about losing their jobs.

Linda: Professor Leaver, that was very interesting. Thank you for talking to me about your work.

Unit 2

Track 4

Speaker 1

Hi, I'm **Timothy Neo** and I'd like to tell you about the personal assistant service I run in Singapore. What does a personal assistant do? Well, in our busy society more and more people don't have enough time to do all the things they have to do. So they can hire me and I'll organize things for them. If they want to have errands done, I can do them. I'll pick up their clothes from the dry-cleaner, take their parcels to the post office, or reserve theater tickets. I have to be flexible, but I don't always do everything myself. For example, if someone wants to have their apartment cleaned, I can organize a cleaner. If they want to give a party, I hire a party service. It's a very creative job and a lot of fun.

Speaker 2

Hello. I'm **Emily Tan**. Everyday almost thirty office workers in Kuala Lumpur eat a freshly cooked lunch, thanks to my husband Arnab and me. Arnab grew up in India, in Mumbai, where every day hundreds of so-called *dabbawala* transport fresh food from homes or central kitchens to offices in the city. That's where we got the idea for our lunch delivery service. A lot of people don't want to eat unhealthy cafeteria food or buy street food, so they have home-cooked food delivered to their offices. Arnab and I do the planning and shopping together. I do the cooking and Arnab delivers the meals. Our business is booming and there are fewer problems than we expected. Most new customers come on recommendation, so we think we must be doing something right!

Speaker 3

My name's **Sayaka Okazaki** and I run my own translating business. Many of my clients want to have personal documents translated into English. And a lot of foreign companies get their product brochures translated into Japanese – they are my best customers. My business also offers translations from German and French into Japanese, but I don't do them myself. I get them done by freelance translators. I have to choose my co-workers carefully because my reputation depends on the quality and speed of our work. We have to be reliable. I don't make a lot of money because I prefer to do fewer translations and do them well.

Speaker 4

I'm **Vincent Chen** and I run a party service in Taipei. Busy people who like to give parties but have little time, get their parties organized by party services like mine. I don't prepare the food myself. I have it prepared in a good restaurant and get it delivered. I get the drinks delivered too. It's more convenient. But I take care of everything else myself. I had a few difficulties setting up the business, but now I have regular customers who recommend me to their friends. Finding new customers is the least of my problems. My main problem is keeping the high standards I've set for myself. I want to be the best in the business.

Before I started my party service, I worked in a bank. I earn less money now, but I enjoy my job much more.

Track 5

Nora: Thank you for a calling the Coffee Bean Company. My name's Nora. How can I help you?

Caller: Hi, I'm calling to find out about a franchise opportunity. Coffee Bean shops is a franchise chain, isn't it?

Nora: That's right, sir. So you want to open a coffee shop?

Caller: No, my wife and I already run a coffee shop, but we want to call it Coffee Bean. How do we apply?

Nora: OK. Well, it works like this: First I'll take down your information, then I'll have some forms sent to you by email. You have to fill them out, fax or mail them back to us, and then one of our representatives in your country will contact you.

Caller: And how long does that take?

Nora: Usually less than a week after we receive the forms.

Caller: OK. What information do you want right now?

Nora: First of all, your name.

Caller: It's Sands, that's S-A-N-D-S. The first name is Charlie. C-H-A-R-L-I-E.

Nora: Mr. Charlie Sands. And your phone number, Mr. Sands?

Caller: It's area code 818 and 172-6354.

Nora: Thank you. And your email address?

Caller: Chas – that's C-H-A-S minus sands at icloud dot com.

Nora: Let me repeat that: chas minus sands at icloud dot com.

Caller: Correct.

Nora: OK. I'm going to send you a test email to make sure I've got it right.

Caller: Um, let me ask you, where can I find out more about franchising? I mean, I want to know exactly how it functions. There's very little information on your website.

Nora: Our rep will give you all the information you need when he contacts you, but if you like, I can get some information material emailed to you in advance.

Caller: That would be great. So you'll have some stuff sent and the next step will be that a rep calls me.

Nora: That's right.

Caller: What kind of things will they want to know?

Nora: Basically they want to know if you have a head for business. But you're already running a business,

so that should be no problem. Now has my test email arrived yet?

Caller: Uh, yes, here it is. Thanks.

Nora: Good. Now is there anything else I can do for you?

Caller: No, that's it. You've been very helpful.

Nora: Thank you. Good-bye and have a nice day.

Track 6

Sayaka: Okazaki Translation Service. How can I help you?

Caller: Oh, you speak English. That's good. Um, I'm calling about a translation: I'd like to have our company report translated into Japanese. Could you tell me something about your service – like, what it costs and how long it would take?

Sayaka: Well, that depends on how long and how difficult the text is.

Caller: It's a 10-page brochure and it's not very difficult. So what would it cost?

Sayaka: I'm afraid I can't say until I have seen a sample page.

Caller: Hmm. I have another question: Can we trust you with confidential documents? I mean, our report is really very confidential.

Sayaka: Of course, I can guarantee that your report will be safe with us. We deal with confidential documents every day.

Caller: So let me see if I've got this right: I have to send you a sample page and then you can tell me exactly what it'll cost.

Sayaka: Exactly.

Caller: So can you give the email address I should send it to?

Sayaka: It's T-S at okazaki dot com

Caller: Let me read that back: T-S at okazaki dot com

Sayaka: Correct. So I'll expect your email. What was the name?

Caller: I'd rather not say at the moment. I'd like to talk to some other agencies first and . . .

Track 7

Ben: BJ-Workwear, Ben Johnson speaking. How can I help you?

Nancy: Hi, Ben. It's Nancy Green from the Clean Machine Company. How are you, Ben?

Ben: Fine, Nancy. And you? How's business?

Nancy: It's good, Ben. We're expanding and taking on new cleaners. That's why I'm calling. I need some work clothes, and I want to be sure you've got everything in stock.

Ben: What do you need exactly?

Nancy: Well, we need twenty aprons – ten red for the women and ten blue for the men.

Ben: Small, medium, or large?

Nancy: Let's say the red ones medium, the blue ones large.

Ben: Yes, we have them all in stock. They're on special this month, $10 each.

Nancy: Good. Then I need ten ladies' blouses – white ones. Five small, five medium; and ten white T-shirts, five medium and five large. What do they cost?

Ben: The blouses are $20 each and $15 each for the T-shirts. Is that okay?

Nancy: That's fine. Now I need some rubber gloves: 25 pink pairs in medium and 25 blue pairs in large – the $2 ones I had last time.

Ben: 50 pairs of rubber gloves at $2 a pair. All in stock, Nancy. It's your lucky day.

Nancy: Is the order big enough for a quantity discount, Ben?

Ben: Well, I can offer you a 5 percent discount on the total price.

Nancy: Thanks, Ben. Listen, I'll put all that in writing and mail my order to you today.

Ben: Great. I'll have everything sent tomorrow, and you should have the delivery within three days. Have a nice day, Nancy. Bye.

Track 8

Mike: California Wine Shop. Mike Wilson speaking. How can I help you?

Vincent: Hi, Mike. It's Vincent Chen from Chen's Party Service.

Mike: Hi, Vincent. How are you doing?

Vincent: Good. And you?

Mike: Yeah, fine. What can I do for you today, Vincent?

Vincent: Well, I'm organizing a big party next weekend, Mike, and I'd like you to deliver the drinks.

Mike: No problem, Vincent. What do you need exactly?

Vincent: Let's start with the soft drinks. Can you send me a dozen bottles of mineral water – the one-point-five liter ones I had last time at 20 dollars a bottle?

Mike: Twelve bottles of mineral water, one-point-five liter bottles. What about fruit juice? We have mango juice and orange juice on special this week – 35 dollars a can.

Vincent: Right. I'll take twenty cans of the mango. And wine? Have you got any on special?

Mike: We have some great Californian red wine at 400 dollars a bottle, and white at 380.

Vincent: I'll take five of each. And two dozen cans of beer.

Mike: Imported or Taiwanese? Taiwanese is much cheaper at 30 dollars a can.

Vincent: Taiwanese is fine. Well, that's all. Can you give us the usual quantity discount, Mike?

Mike: Sure. I can give you a 5 percent discount on the total price. But could you confirm the order in writing?

Vincent: No problem, Mike. I'll send you an email today. And of course, I'll pay within ten days as usual. OK?

Mike: Fine, Vincent – and good luck with your party!

Track 9

1 **A** The man is having pizza delivered.
  B The woman is delivering pizza.
  C The woman is having pizza delivered.
  D The pizza delivery costs nothing.

2 **A** The man is asking for information at the station.
   B The man wants to know when his train leaves.
   C The man wants to know when his flight leaves.
   D A lot of people are reading the information board.

Track 〔10〕

Example: Which time is better for you – morning or afternoon?
   A I'm free after lunch.
   B Sorry, I've no idea what the time is.
   C OK, I'll be there on time.

1 How should we send the delivery?
   A By the end of the week if possible.
   B To our head office on Watergate Street.
   C By courier would be the fastest.

2 Why do you want a loan from the bank?
   A Yes, I saw him in the bank.
   B We want to buy a new car.
   C The bank closes at four.

3 I've finished the report. Would you like a copy?
   A No, thanks. I don't have time to read it.
   B No, thanks. I don't drink coffee.
   C Yes, I really like them.

4 How many hours a day do you work?
   A Six days a week.
   B Very much.
   C Between seven and nine.

Track 〔11〕

Imagine an international marketing company is doing research in your country. You have agreed to take part in a television interview about your leisure time.

Question 1 How much leisure time do you have each week?
Question 2 What kinds of things do you like to do in your leisure time?
Question 3 Describe your favorite leisure time activity.

Unit 3
Track 〔12〕

I'd like to start today by looking at some basic ideas in marketing. Marketing is all about putting the right product at the right price in the right place at the right time. This mix is known as the "the four Ps."

The first two Ps stand for product and price – that means providing customers with a product at a price they feel is fair. Informing customers about the product and persuading them to buy it is known as promotion. The fourth P stands for place, which is about making the product easily available.

Let's now look more closely at each of the four Ps. A product can be goods or services – a new car or a vacation in the sun. The product has to look special so that people will want to have it. That's why the image of a product is just as important as the product itself. But we'll come back to that when we talk about promotion.

Now for price. The price must make it possible for your product to compete effectively with similar products. So, even if it's expensive, customers must feel they are getting value for their money, or they won't buy your product.

Promotion means presenting your product to the customers and convincing them that they want to have it. You must create an image for your product. Who is it for? Should it be traditional or trendy, a luxury brand or a mass-market product? Packaging is important and so is a well-designed logo. Then you must make your product known, for example, by advertising via TV commercials, webvertising, print advertising, or billboards.

Finally place. Your product must be easily available to the people who want to buy it. There is no point in having an expensive promotion campaign if the customer can't find your product.

So your most important questions are: What needs does my customer have and

how can my product or service satisfy those needs?
What is the value of the product or service to the customer?
What is the best way to get my advertising message across to my target group?
Where will buyers look for my product or service?

Market research will help you to find out the answers. And that will be our topic next week.

Now, are there any questions . . . ?

Track 13

Speaker 1
I stopped buying expensive clothes years ago. I like keeping up with the latest fashions, so I never wear things more than a couple of times. That's why there's no point in paying a lot for stuff.

Speaker 2
I saw a TV commercial for a watch that I really liked, but I couldn't get one anywhere. My local store didn't sell it, and online shopping sites told me that the watch wasn't yet available. What's the point of advertising something you can't get a hold of!

Speaker 3
We paid a lot for this sofa, but it's beautifully made and we've had it for years. The kids have jumped on it, the dog has slept on it, and it still looks good. That's what I call real quality.

Speaker 4
The phone company had a marvelous booth at the trade show. They also had really helpful and well-informed staff who pointed out the advantages of different models and helped me to decide which one was best for me. I ordered one on the spot.

Track 14

Misaki: Hi, Dave. Hey, I like your new sneakers. They're PTs, aren't they?
Dave: Yes, Misaki, PT is my favorite brand. They make me look cool!

Misaki: Miguel, what do you think? Why aren't you wearing sneakers that make you look cool?
Miguel: Because I always buy the cheapest sneakers I can find. I don't need to look cool – I am cool!
Dave: Ha, ha. Seriously, PT sneakers are expensive, but they're really good value for money. That's why I buy them.
Miguel: Come on, you've been brainwashed by advertising. You just want to impress people.
Dave: So what? Wearing a logo with a positive image makes me feel good.
Miguel: Well, I'm sure I don't want to be a walking advertisement for some brand name!
Misaki: Don't you ever buy famous brands, Miguel?
Miguel: Only if a product has some special feature that I want. Usually I prefer cheaper no-name products. With brand names you often pay for the name and not the quality.
Misaki: I don't think that's true. Famous brands want to keep their good reputation. I buy them because I can rely on them for good quality.
Dave: Misaki's right. That's exactly why I prefer brand names. Anyway, how come millions of people want to have the same product? They can't all be wrong.
Miguel: Because companies spend billions on promotion and placement, that's why – not because the product is better.
Misaki: But I like having the same things that my friends have.
Miguel: Misaki, you are just so boring.

Track 15

available	luxury
commercial	marketing
convincing	packaging
customer	promotion
effectively	similar
expensive	traditional
important	vacation

Hi, this is Rob Hall from Asia-Pacific Business Specialists. Not knowing gift-giving customs when traveling to other countries can be bad for business, so I'd like to give you some tips about giving and receiving gifts in the business world.

In many countries such as in North America and the UK, gift giving is rare in the business world. In fact, it may be seen as a bribe. This is also the case in countries like Malaysia, and in Singapore government employees are not allowed to accept gifts. In many other Asian countries, however, gift giving has a central place in business tradition.

Let's start with Japan. Here exchanging gifts is very important, and gifts are often exchanged at the end of the first meeting. Let your Japanese partners give their gifts first, then present yours with both hands. Make sure you have a gift for everyone present. Bow and tell your partners: "This is just a small gift." Even if the gift is modest, it should look good, so attractive wrapping is important. The Japanese may refuse a gift once or twice before accepting it.

The Chinese tradition, on the other hand, is to refuse a gift three times! Don't be frustrated, play the game. As in Japan, make sure you have a gift for everyone and present it with both hands. Never give an expensive gift until you have a firm relationship with your business partners. In fact, some companies forbid employees to accept any gifts. Avoid giving one of something. Chinese philosophy stresses harmony and balance, so give things in pairs, for example two books or two pictures.

In Indonesia, business gifts are generally not exchanged, but small gifts may be given to colleagues after business is completed. It is impolite to refuse a gift. Gifts are not opened in front of the giver unless there is some kind of ceremony. The same applies to China and Japan, whereas in the United States and the UK you are expected to open your gift and express your appreciation.

Gift-giving in Thailand is more westernized and less formal than in other Asian countries. As in Indonesia, it would be impolite to refuse a gift. Give and receive a gift with your right hand and offer a "wai". Do not open the gift. Put it aside and open it in private.

So, that's all for today. I hope that knowing the gift etiquette of your business partners will help to make your meetings a success. Good luck!

Unit 4

Kristin: What's wrong, Amy? You look rather down.

Amy: I'm really frustrated, Kristin. I just don't look forward to coming to work anymore.

Kristin: But you always said that you loved your job.

Amy: I do, but I can't get along with the new project manager. He's making my life miserable and it's getting me down.

Kristin: You mean Ken Tsai? But he seems really nice.

Amy: Perhaps he is if you don't have to work with him.

Kristin: What's the problem exactly?

Amy: Oh, I can't do anything right. He always seems to find me out at the wrong moment. Like yesterday. I was calling a friend on my cell phone when he came into the office. He was angry and he told me off. He said I was wasting the company's time on private phone calls.

Kristin: Sorry, Amy, but he's right.

Amy: Oh, I know. But it was only a quick call. Anyway, he asked me to prepare a report before lunchtime. So I started to write the report and I was working on some statistics when my computer crashed!

Kristin: Yes, we had problems in the sales department too. The company is trying out a new system.

Amy: Right. So when he asked for the report, I told him that it wasn't finished. He was really annoyed and stormed out of the office.

Kristin: But it wasn't your fault.

Amy: No, but obviously he blamed me and he didn't give me a chance to explain. Well, after lunch, I started working on the report again, but I was so nervous I kept making mistakes. Then I heard someone come into my office, and when I turned around, Ken was standing behind me, looking at my computer screen.

Kristin: And what did he say?

Amy: He asked me if I knew what I was doing. He made me feel totally incompetent!

Kristin: Oh dear. That sounds bad. Look, Amy, would it help to talk to him and tell him that his behavior makes you nervous?

Amy: I wanted to do that yesterday before I left the office, but he said he didn't have time. Anyway, I've had enough. I can't put up with it any longer. I'm going to ask for a transfer to another department.

Kristin: Well, that's probably a good idea. Perhaps you could come to my department. We have a really good working atmosphere.

Amy: That'd be great. I've got an appointment with the Human Resources department this afternoon. Keep your fingers crossed for me, Kristin.

Kristin: Yes, Amy, you can count on me.

Track 18

Sue: Good morning listeners. This is Sue Harris welcoming you to our program *Working Abroad*. Our guest today is Stan Walker, who works as a project manager in Bangkok. Welcome to the program, Stan.

Stan: Thanks for inviting me, Sue.

Sue: Stan, you're from Australia. What made you decide to go to work in Thailand?

Stan: My company in Perth asked for volunteers to set up a branch in Bangkok. I thought it would be a challenge – and it certainly has been.

Sue: What was your major problem when you started?

Stan: Learning how to be the boss of Thai employees.

Sue: Why was that?

Stan: Because I had to learn a whole new style of management, and at first I made a lot of the cultural mistakes that "farang" – or foreign – bosses often make.

Sue: Can you give us an example?

Stan: Well, in Australia we prefer team-based decisions, but I had to learn that Thai employees expect their boss to make the decisions, then tell them what to do. I also learned that "yes" doesn't always mean "yes." It can also mean "maybe" or even "no." At first, when I was giving instructions, the employees smiled and nodded. When I asked them if they understood, they said "yes," but later it turned out that they didn't know what they had to do; they just wanted to please me. So I learned to ask them to repeat my instructions.

Sue: It's often said that "farangs" are too focused on results. Is that right?

Stan: Yes, that's another point I wanted to mention. Thais are very sociable and it's important to build relationships with your employees. Go out with them for lunch or to a karaoke bar. Have some fun and try to find the right balance between business targets and relationships.

Sue: What else did you have to learn about Thai business culture?

Stan: I had to learn not to show my emotions and especially not to get angry. Thai people are generally peaceful people, and getting angry in public is not acceptable. If you do, they'll see it as a weakness and you'll lose their respect.

Sue: Is that what is called "losing face"?

Stan: Yes. People lose face when they lose their self-respect or the respect of others. So you must do everything you can to keep face – both yours and other people's. That's why you shouldn't criticize your staff or point out their mistakes in public. Open conflict is taboo, so you should try to solve problems behind closed doors.

Sue: Do you have any other tips how foreign managers can improve their relationship to their Thai employees?

Stan: Yes. Take time to read about Thai culture and learn at least the basics of the Thai language. Your reward will be a happy and successful stay in this wonderful country.

Track 19

Writing summaries is a very important skill in today's business world. You may need to summarize articles or reports, make a summary business plan, summarize the results of meetings or the arguments for and against something. So let's take a look at the best way to write a summary.

Before you even begin to write, you should read the text at least twice. The first time you read don't worry about details, just read to get a general understanding – what we call the gist of the text.

Before you read a second time, think of who you are writing the summary for. What will they want to know? What information is important to them? Then read the text carefully and highlight the important parts.

The third step is to write sentences based on the parts that you highlighted – write only the main ideas and leave out the details. Use lists and bullet points to make your summary short and simple. As a heading you can write: *Summary of . . .* and tell the readers where they can find the original report in case they want to read it in full.

When you are finished, you should read your summary again to see if there are any sentences that you can make even shorter. In the final step, you should check your summary very carefully and perhaps get someone else to check it. Four eyes are always better than two!

Track 20

Conversation 1

Man: I've finished writing my proposal for the new marketing strategy.

Woman: Well done. But we'll have to discuss it with Ken Tsai before we give it to the director.

Man: OK. But Ken said he didn't have time to discuss it this morning. He's in a meeting in the director's office.

Woman: Oh, OK. So, let's leave it now and go to the cafeteria for lunch. Then we'll go to his office this afternoon.

Question 1 What will the speakers do first?
Question 2 What will the speakers do last?
Question 3 Where will the speakers discuss the proposal?

Conversation 2

Woman: My co-worker, Sandra, is getting me down. She was friendly to me when I first joined the company, but now she's changed.

Man: Sandra? But she's a really nice person, and she gets along well with everyone. What has she done to upset you?

Woman: Well, she's really lazy, and I have to do all the work. She doesn't take down phone messages, and my customers get angry. But the worst thing is she tells tales about me to the boss.

Man: Mmm, I think the best solution would be to talk to Sandra. If that doesn't help, you can always ask for a transfer.

Question 1 What does the woman dislike most about Sandra?
Question 2 What does the man say about Sandra?
Question 3 What does the man think the best solution would be for the woman?

Unit 5

Track 21

Donna: Peter, I have to set up a videoconference meeting next week with our Thailand office and I need to know when you're available.

Peter: OK, a meeting with Khun Anocha, right?

Donna: Yes, Khun Anocha, you, and Susan. Will you be free on Thursday?

Peter: Thursday? Hmm … I had planned to work from home on Thursday, but I suppose I could change that.

Donna: There's no need to change it. Do you have access to Skype at home?

Peter: Oh yes, of course. Skype! OK then. Let's see if we can arrange something for Thursday afternoon, via Skype.

Donna: Great. Thank goodness for technology, huh?

Peter: Absolutely! I don't know how I would survive without it. Have you spoken to Khun Anocha yet?

Donna: Yes, I texted her today because she hadn't replied to my email. She said she hadn't received it. I need to check what the problem is.

Peter: Uh, maybe you sent it to the wrong person. I've done something like that before! Have I told you about when I was flying back from Thailand last month? I had a two-hour stopover in Singapore, so I sent my wife a quick text message to tell her I was OK.

Donna: Uh-huh.

Peter: And I said something like "Hi, darling, I'm on my way. See you soon."

Donna: So what happened?

Peter: Well, she didn't answer, but a friend of mine did!

Donna: What? Why?

Peter: He'd received the text I thought I'd sent to my wife! I realized I'd sent the text to the wrong person!

Donna: Oh no! That's awful. What did he say?

Peter: Not much, I quickly called him to explain, but he was too busy laughing nonstop!

Donna: That's so funny! Well, I suppose we need to be more careful!

Peter: That's true. If you ask me, people aren't cautious enough with all these new communication media. How do you see it?

Donna: I couldn't agree more. Everything happens so fast and I suppose some people find state-of-the-art technology a bit confusing!

Peter: Some people? You mean me, right? I guess I'm a bit helpless sometimes.

Donna: No, no. I disagree. In my opinion, you're pretty good with technology. You just need to check before you click "send"!

Track 22

Good morning, this is Jackie Thompson with the Asia-Pacific business news.

Japan: The number of jobs available in June has increased to the highest level in more than three years. At the end of last year, the unemployment rate had increased to a record level, but as the economy has improved, companies have become more willing to recruit new employees. According to the Ministry of Health, Labor, and Welfare, there are now 94 jobs available for 100 job seekers.

Singapore: Changi airport handled a record 4.5 million passengers last month – an increase of 4 percent compared with May of last year. By the end of May this year, 31 million passengers had used the airport, 4.9 percent more than the same period last year. The airport has been in the hands of the Changi Airport Group since July 2009. Since then, passenger numbers have increased by 11 percent and revenue has doubled.

Malaysia: The government has announced plans to develop tourist attractions close to the Malaysia-Thailand border. The area already has a duty-free shopping center, but Malaysia plans to add other attractions to encourage Thais across the border to spend money in Malaysia. "This will create jobs for local residents," said a government spokesman.

And finally news from Australia: The country's oldest paper money will stay in Australia after it fetched a record price at an auction in Sydney. The ten-shilling note was one of only a hundred issued on April 8 in 1817 – the day the Bank of New South Wales opened in Australia. The rare bank note was found in a private collection and sold for a record $334,000.

Track 23

businessman, computer virus, credit card, fifteen-year-old, job seeker, movie star, phone number, smartphone, time zone, traffic jam, travel agent, T-shirt, website

Track 24

Speaker 1

In my country, when we meet business partners for the first time, we pay attention to the way they dress, their body language and gestures. We usually avoid direct questions. With co-workers, it's important to cooperate and work as a team. It's not a good idea to criticize your co-workers because they will lose face. Saving face is very important in my culture. Anyway, people usually know when they've made a mistake, and they'll try harder next time. It's important to have good relationships and an atmosphere of harmony, so we try to avoid conflict. You have to think about people's feelings. You have to trust your business partners, so we don't always ask for things in writing. For us tradition is very important.

Speaker 2

When we first meet business partners in my country, we ask "Where are you from? What do you do?" and other direct questions. In my culture we give our opinions, and if somebody doesn't agree with them, they say so. And sometimes we criticize each other. Telling people what you think will help them to do a better job next time. Conflict is not personal. We separate the person from the problem. The business world is pretty competitive. We like to focus on the task and expect to take individual responsibility for what we do. In business, facts are more important than feelings, and decisions are made on the basis of information. We prefer to have important things in writing. It's our way of doing business.

Unit 6

Track 25

Rob: OK, let's get started. Does everyone have a copy of the agenda? Good. The main purpose of the meeting is to discuss the annual sales conference in September this year. But first let's have an update on any problems since our last meeting. Nuri, could you take the minutes?

Nuri: Sure, Rob.

Rob: OK. So let's take the first point on the agenda. Jed, would you like to begin with an update?

Jed: Thanks, Rob, Well, in the past two weeks we . . .

Rob: OK, let's move on to the next point on the agenda – the location of the sales conference. Dinda, you're going to check out possible venues. What are the most important things we need to think about?

Dinda: Well, the main priority is to find a hotel with all the facilities we need at a price we want to pay. First the rooms. We'll need a conference room for about 60 participants, a number of smaller rooms for workshops and training sessions, a room for breaks, and an executive room for senior staff. And of course, we need accommodations for the participants.

Rob: OK, but may I remind you to keep an eye on the costs. We must stick to our budget because—

Jed: Can I interrupt there, Rob?

Rob: Just let me finish, please, Jed. We have a budget of $2,000 per participant – that includes everything – venue, transportation, catering, accommodation – everything. Are you with me, Dinda?

Dinda: Yes, Rob, I've got it.

Jed: But we want the participants to enjoy themselves as well as working hard. The hotel should be at least four stars and have a good restaurant and some leisure facilities – or there should be some facilities nearby, a golf course, for example. Don't you think so, Dinda?

Dinda: OK, Jed, I'll bear in mind your favorite sport when I'm looking for a suitable hotel!

Jed: I'll help you to do some research if you want.

Dinda: Thanks, Jed, but can we get back to the main point? We need a hotel that can also offer us state-of-the-art technical facilities. And it mustn't be too far from an international airport, as most people will arrive by air. A shuttle service from the airport would be useful. So, if I can just summarize: we need a hotel that's near an airport and has suitable rooms, technical and leisure facilities, and—

Rob: May I just come in there, Dinda? Have you started your research?

Dinda: Yes. I've already found five hotels that meet our requirements and asked them to quote us a price. Then I'm going to choose the three best and send a questionnaire to the participants to find out which one they prefer.

Rob: Good. Now, who's going to organize the workshop registrations?

Akmal: I'll take care of that, Rob. I'll probably just update last year's registration form. I've already told the sales department to put together a mailing list. I think the deadline for registration should be six weeks before the conference.

Nuri: Are you saying that we need registrations six weeks in advance, Akmal? Isn't that rather long?

Dinda: Akmal's right. I think we'll need six weeks. We'll need to confirm the final bookings, participants will have to book their flights–

Rob: OK. Now, I asked Nuri if she wanted to prepare the program and organize the speakers again this year. Is that still OK with you, Nuri?

Nuri: Yes, I've already contacted the most popular ones from last year. I asked them whether they could come again this year. I'm waiting for their replies. And, of course, we're going to invite some new speakers too.

Rob: OK. And I advise you to check their technical requirements and coordinate with Dinda about . . .

Track 26

Rob: . . . so we all agree that Jed will be responsible for organizing the leisure program including some team-building activities. OK, I think we've covered everything. Are there any other questions?

Dinda: I have one more question. Are we going to hire interpreters?

Rob: No, they're too expensive. The working language will be English. Participants can organize their own interpreters or translators if they want to. Well, I'm afraid we're running out of time. Before we finish, I'd like to summarize the action points that we've agreed on so that Nuri can put them in the minutes. Dinda, you're going to get offers from five hotels and prepare a questionnaire. Akmal, you're going to take care of the registrations. Jed is going to organize the leisure program and help Dinda with her research. Nuri is going to organize the speakers and write up today's minutes with the action points. Can you let us have them by the end of the week, Nuri?

Nuri: No problem, I'll do them today and let you have them tomorrow morning.

Rob: Good. The last item on the agenda is AOB – any other business. Is there anything anyone would like to talk about? No? Well, if there is nothing else to discuss, the meeting is closed. Please follow up your action points and bring your results to the next meeting. I suggest meeting in two weeks, same time, same place – I'll confirm by email in the next few days. Thanks everyone. You've come up with some great ideas.

Track 27

Co-workers, I'd like to give you a short presentation of the venue for the next sales conference. We've chosen the Bamboo Conference Hotel in Hanoi. It's a five-star hotel and has 250 rooms. There are twelve large and small meeting rooms, all air-conditioned and fully equipped with state-of-the-art technology. It is located right in the center of the city's government and business district. A 10-minute walk takes you to the main tourist attractions such as the Tortoise Pagoda, St. Joseph's Cathedral, and Hanoi Opera House. Hanoi Central Railway Station is a 10-minute drive, and Hanoi International Airport is 28 kilometers from the hotel. The hotel provides a shuttle-bus service to and from the airport.

The price for the three-day conference is $1,800 per participant, which includes meals and entertainment. If you check out guest reviews, the only negative comments are that the drinks are very expensive and the service at reception is slow.

Track 28

We're looking for a venue for our annual sales conference in September. We plan to arrive on Friday, September 12, and leave on Monday, September 15. We need well-equipped meeting rooms and accommodations for about 50 participants. I have a couple of questions I hope you can answer.

Question 1 How much does a conference room for 25 people cost per day?

Question 2 What leisure-time facilities do you offer?

Question 3 Could you tell me something about your catering and restaurant facilities?

Unit 7

Track 29

Good morning. My name is Nicole Shaw and I'm here today to talk to you about what makes a good presentation. It's no wonder speakers get so nervous when you think that speaking in public is one of the top five fears – alongside snakes, spiders, small spaces, and heights! But believe me, it's something that can be learned, and if you follow my advice, you'll find it a lot easier.

I'm going to divide my presentation into four parts. First, I'd like to talk about planning and preparation. My next point will be about opening your presentation and some tips on giving the presentation itself. Then I'll give you some ideas for closing your presentation, and finally I'd like to talk about clothes and body language.

So let's start with planning and preparation. It's so important to research your topic carefully. Don't write down every word, just some key notes and useful phrases. Before your presentation, make sure the room has been prepared and the technical equipment has been checked. Any handouts you want to distribute must be photocopied in advance. Check that you have enough copies. It's such an easy thing to forget.

Start your presentation by introducing yourself and your topic. Don't read from your notes. Look at your audience. An audience likes to be entertained, so make your talk interesting. Make a few spontaneous comments and tell a couple of jokes.

Tell the audience at the beginning what the structure of your talk will be. Give "signposts" such as "first," "next," and "finally" while you talk so that your listeners can follow you better. Do you remember I told you at the beginning that my talk has four parts and I told you what they would be?

Speak clearly, slowly, and loudly enough so that you can be heard and understood by everyone.

Questions should be saved for the end of your talk so you can do your presentation without interruptions.

Use visuals – people understand much better when they can see things. But don't stand in front of the screen and block the view when visuals are being shown! That's such a common mistake that inexperienced speakers make.

You can close your presentation with a summary of your main points. In other words: you start a presentation by telling your audience what you are going to say, then you say it, and you finish by telling them what you said.

Finally, I'd like to say something about body language and clothes. Don't underestimate the importance of appearance in today's business world. Stand up straight, look confident, smile, and make eye contact with your audience. The right clothes – whether it's casual jeans or formal jacket and dark trousers – will depend on the situation and on your company's dress code. In any case, you should aim to look professional, or you might not be taken seriously.

Well, that brings me to the end of my presentation. Thank you for your attention. Now, if anyone has any questions, I'll do my best to answer them.

Track 30

1 It was **such a** long presentation and I was **so** bored.
2 The new equipment was **so** expensive, but it was **such a** big improvement.
3 This job is **so** hard and there's **so** much to do.
4 Bangkok is **such a** great city and it's **so** exciting.
5 My co-workers are **so** nice. We're **such a** good team.
6 My boss is **such a** nice person and **such a** good boss.
7 **Such a** lot of people have a smartphone now because they are **so** cheap.

Track 31

Chen: Well, that brings me to the end of my presentation. Now if anyone has any questions . . . . No? OK, then I'll finish here. Thank you for your attention.
Nicole: OK, everyone. So what do you think of Chen's presentation? Let's have your comments. Yes, Suling?
Suling: Well, I think it was a really interesting presentation and clearly it had been well researched, but you forgot to introduce yourself at the beginning, Chen.
Chen: Did I? I was feeling so nervous. I'm not very confident speaking in front of other people.
Nicole: That's just a question of practice, Chen. The more you do it, the

more relaxed you'll be. Any other comments? Yes, Luke?
Luke: Well, I think the visuals that were shown were really great. But, Chen, I really think you need to speak more slowly. You kind of raced through it.
Chen: Did I?
Nicole: Yes, I think that's a fair comment. Slow down, and remember to look at your listeners.
Suling: I agree. You didn't really make enough eye contact with us, but you didn't look at your notes much – which was good. I really liked the way you opened the presentation with a little joke. That was nice.
Nicole: That's right. Now was there anything else?
Luke: Yeah, I thought you structured the presentation really well, Chen. The signposts you gave us were such a great help.
Suling: Yes, and I thought it was good that you gave us lots of examples. But that made the talk a bit too long.
Chen: Yes, I underestimated the time I would need. But anyway, thanks for the feedback everyone. It's really helpful.
Nicole: So, on the whole you did a good job, Chen. Thanks a lot – and keep practicing!

Track 32

My name is Nicole Shaw and I'm here today to talk to you about what makes a good presentation.

I'm going to divide my presentation into four parts.

First, I'd like to talk about planning and preparation. My next point will be about opening your presentation and some tips on giving the presentation itself. Then I'll give you some ideas for closing your presentation.

Finally, I'd like to talk about clothes and body language.

So let's start with planning and preparation.

Well, that brings me to the end of my presentation. Thank you for your attention. Now, if anyone has any questions, I'll do my best to answer them.

Track 33

Hi, this is Rob Hall from Asia-Pacific Business Specialists. Today I'd like to talk to you about the right clothes for doing business in the Asia-Pacific region. In general, if you don't know a company's dress code, business dress should be conservative and low-key – no bright colors, for example, and no mini-skirts and low necklines for women. When you get to know your business partners better, you might dress differently.

So let's take a closer look at some Asia-Pacific countries. We'll begin in Thailand, where ties and long-sleeved shirts are standard office wear for men and blouse, skirt, and jacket for women. This may sound uncomfortable in such a hot climate, but the air-conditioning is often set to a low temperature. When visiting someone's home, you will be asked to remove your shoes, so make sure you don't have any holes in your socks!

In Indonesia business dress is often casual because of the extreme heat. Standard office wear for men includes dark pants and a light-colored, long-sleeved shirt and tie without a jacket. However, a jacket and tie are still the best choice for a businessman visiting Jakarta for the first time. Many Indonesian men wear an open-necked, long-sleeved batik shirt to the office and Western businessmen can do the same once they know the company's dress code. Women should wear blouses that cover their upper arms, and skirts should not be too short.

Most companies in Australia have a dress code. Banking and finance are the most conservative with a dark suit and white shirt for men and a skirt or pants suit and a white blouse for women. Some companies have "casual Friday," when employees can dress in a more relaxed way. But even then there are limits, and jeans or shorts would not be acceptable.

Some companies in Japan have also introduced "casual Friday." In fact, business dress in Japan has become less conservative than it was in the past. A former prime minister recommended not wearing ties in the summer to save on air-conditioning costs, and this has continued in many companies. But I still recommend that you wear a jacket and tie on your first visit. If your business partners are not wearing jackets, you can ask politely if you can take yours off – but it's better to leave the tie on! Women should wear formal clothes to be taken seriously and win respect.

And finally, the Philippines. A light-weight, formal shirt called a "Barong Tagalog" is often worn by businessmen in formal meetings. You should wear a long-sleeved shirt and tie, but not a suit. That would be too formal, and you would not be very comfortable in the climate there. Light suits or dresses are suitable for women.

So, that is all I want to tell you today. Thank you for your attention. Now, does any one have any questions . . .?

Unit 8

Track 34

Ethan: Good morning, listeners. Welcome to *The World of Work*. My name is Ethan Thomas. For most Asians, the definition of success is getting a good qualification and a good job. But while many young people still dream of becoming accountants, computer programmers, or engineers, more and more people in Taiwan today are choosing non-academic jobs. With me are Florence Wu from the Taipei Vocational Training Center, and Sam Kao, who left his job as an engineer to work in a car repair shop. Florence, why is there a new interest in non-academic or practical work?

Florence: One reason is that a vocational skill can often be more useful in the job market than academic training. Also more young people these days believe they can be just as happy as a mechanic or an electrician as a teacher or a journalist.

Ethan: Sam, why did you change to a completely different type of work? Was it money?

Sam: If I had wanted to earn money, I would have started work at 18 and not studied for four years. No, money has never been my main motivation.

Ethan: So what was the reason?

Sam: Job satisfaction! I wouldn't have changed my job if I'd been happy. My old job in a high-tech company was very demanding. I had to travel a lot and work long hours with no overtime pay. Now I have fixed hours and overtime is paid by the hour. I didn't use to look forward to work, but I do now.

Ethan: Did you use to worry a lot about your work?

Sam: Yes, I did. And I used to take work home. Now, when I leave the workshop, I can close the door behind me and forget about it.

Ethan: Florence, is Sam typical?

Florence: Well, many people who filled in our online questionnaire talked about long hours and the difficulty of finding well-paid jobs in their field. Sixty percent said they would be willing to retrain and change their job. After all, plumbers and technicians are skilled workers too.

Ethan: I heard about someone with a master's degree who took an unskilled job selling fried chicken because he was unable to find anything suitable in his field.

Florence: Yes, I've heard stories like that, but I think that's rather extreme.

Ethan: How did your parents react to your decision, Sam?

Sam: They thought it was a pity because I had a college degree. But now they can see that I'm happy they've accepted it.

Florence: Yes, that's also typical. As the image of vocational training improves, we see more parents willing to let their children do it instead of going to college. I think it's a good development. A college degree *is* special, but it's not the only way to find a job that really suits your personality and that you enjoy doing.

Ethan: Well, thank you both very much for joining us on the program. Now listeners, we'd like to hear your opinion. Our lines are now open. . . .

Track 35

1 I didn't use to organize meetings, but now it's part of my job.
2 Did you use to do more sports?
3 Liu used to earn more money than she does now.
4 Did you use to travel a lot?
5 I used to speak French, but I've forgotten it now.
6 I didn't use to like my boss, but I do now.

Track 36

My name's Alisa Boonliang. I'm an engineer and I work in the U.K. for a large electronics company located near London. I was born in Thailand and I used to work in Bangkok, but my husband is British, so I came to live and work here. I've worked for this company for six years now. I like my job and the working conditions are very good. It's a secure job and the salary is excellent. We are paid for overtime, and we get a bonus once a year. I get five weeks annual paid leave and six weeks sick leave a year if I'm ill. Last year I had a baby and I was on fully paid maternity leave for six weeks before my baby was born.

Fortunately, mine isn't a regular nine-to-five job. We don't have fixed hours, we have flextime, so I can organize my work to fit with our family life. My company is very generous, and when I wanted to travel with my husband last time he went abroad on business, they gave me a month's unpaid leave. I was so grateful. It would have been awful if I hadn't been able to go with him.

And I won't have to worry about money when I'm old. The state provides a pension and my company has its own pension plan. Yes, I'm very satisfied with my company and I think I'm very lucky.

Track 37

1 **A** The electrician is fixing the lights.
  B The woman is in the kitchen.
  C The plumber is fixing the pipes.
  D The technician is doing repairs.

2 **A** The office employee is working hard.
  B The office employee is on leave.
  C The office is crowded today.
  D There are a lot of documents on the desk.

Track 38

Example: Has the letter arrived yet?
  A Yes, It's on your desk.
  B Yes, the ladder's outside.
  C Yes, I'll post it later.

1 What do you do for a living?
  A I don't live here.
  B I'm a secretary.
  C I'm living with my parents.

2 I didn't see you in the office yesterday.
  A I was out of work.
  B I was in work.
  C I was off work.

3 Does she have a nine-to-five job?
  A Yes, she works fixed hours.
  B Yes, she works flextime.
  C No, she works full-time.

4 Is your job demanding?
  A Yes, it's pretty easy.
  B No, it's quite hard.
  C Yes, it's pretty difficult.

Track 39

Hello, this is Kate Wilson. I'm a regular customer in your boutique, and so far I've been pretty satisfied with the stuff I've had from you. But two weeks ago, I bought a very expensive wool dress. I washed it yesterday and of course I followed the instructions on the label. But now it's shrunk. It's so small that I can't wear it. I'm just so disappointed. I didn't expect that from such an expensive item. I'm afraid I don't have the receipt anymore, but I paid for it with my credit card, so it will be on my statement at the end of the month.

Unit 9

Track 40

Lester: You look very cool and casual, Jessica. Haven't you been to work today?

Jessica: Yes, I have. This is our new office dress code. We don't have to wear formal clothes anymore. That way we can keep the air-conditioning at 25 degrees. That helps keep cooling costs down and save energy.

Lester: And who came up with that idea?

Jessica: Felix, my boss. He calculated the company's carbon footprint and was extremely shocked. It was huge. He says if we don't all become more environmentally friendly, we'll destroy the planet.

Lester: Well, I know about carbon footprints, but I've never checked mine. I try not to waste energy, anyway. I always switch off machines when I'm not using them. It really makes a difference to my energy bills. They would be much higher if I left everything on standby.

Jessica: Right. And you should use a train or bus to go to work and not your car – or even better, walk! Do you know how much CO_2 commuters produce? *Billions* of tons a year! I wouldn't have known that if Felix hadn't told me. He's an expert on the environment.

Lester: Hmm, it certainly sounds like it. So what else is your company doing?

Jessica: We've banned plastic cups at the water cooler. Everyone has to use their own cup. We already

Lester: use environmentally friendly office material, and Felix said we would switch to a green cleaning company as soon as possible. We also try to save paper by copying and printing on both sides.

Lester: It's surprising how much paper we still use. People always said that one day we would have paperless offices, but I can't see that happening, can you?

Jessica: Not really. But, when Felix asked us why we printed out so many documents, no one in the office had an answer.

Lester: Perhaps somehow we don't trust our computers!

Jessica: You might be right. Anyway, we're all going to get new laptops at work. Have you any idea how much less energy they consume than standard desktop computers?

Lester: No idea at all.

Jessica: Ninety percent less! Just imagine! Look, Lester, if you want to know what your carbon footprint is, why don't you go online, put "carbon footprint calculator" into your search engine, and check it out? You'll probably get a big surprise!

Lester: Yes, good idea. I think I'll do that, Jessica.

Track 41

Daniel: Welcome to today's discussion about the future of business transportation. My discussion partner today is Mike Anderson, a businessman from the U.K. Mike, globalization means that huge amounts of goods are transported worldwide. But transportation is not without its problems, is it?

Mike: You're right, Daniel. As you know, the first main problem is the pollution of the environment, and the second one is the increasing cost, especially of land transportation. Did you know that it costs more to transport a container 150 kilometers by truck over land in the U.K. than to move the same container 8,000 miles from London to Shanghai by ship?

Daniel: I suppose that's because a truck or a freight train can't carry as many containers as a ship can.

Mike: That's right. So about 90 percent of the world's freight is transported by ship.

Daniel: But there are major environmental concerns, aren't there? The shipping industry produces more carbon dioxide than the rail and air transportation industries together.

Mike: That's true, but now there are some innovations that are helping to reduce the amount of CO_2 that ships are producing. For example, a German company has introduced a new technology so that ships can use wind energy at sea.

Daniel: Yes, and I've also heard about a French project where ships will use a combination of solar power and wave energy.

Mike: Right. Now if they could get such projects off the ground, it would make an enormous contribution to the protection of the environment.

Daniel: But we will still need overland transportation, so what do you think the most important developments in this field will be?

Mike: I'm sure unmanned drones will play an important role in the future. They're relatively cheap and environmentally friendly. They're fast and . . .

Daniel: . . . they can't get stuck in traffic jams. That's a big advantage.

Mike: True. And they can fly for much longer than a human being could pilot a plane or drive a truck or train. In fact, a British drone recently flew more than 82 hours nonstop and broke the world record.

Daniel: So what happens to all the traditional drivers?

Mike: They could retrain and become drone operators! No, seriously, drones are a really interesting development, and I believe that in 10 to 15 years, they'll revolutionize business transportation.

Daniel: I think you're probably right.

Unit 10

Umar: Have you found anything interesting yet, Sumalee?

Sumalee: Yes, I have, Umar. For example, this ad. It says: "Fit-for-Fun: A new exciting fitness training center located in RSU Tower, Bangkok. We are looking for full-time front desk staff to join our team. We offer a friendly and relaxed working atmosphere. Candidates must be self-confident, hardworking, and good with people. Applicants should have a degree and be able to speak English well. Fresh graduates will be considered. Check out our website . . . " etc., etc.

Umar: That sounds good. Your English is great, you're pretty good with people, and you're sporty too.

Sumalee: Yes, I think I'd be good at a job like that. The ad says you can submit a résumé online, and shortlisted candidates will be contacted for an interview. I'd like to apply, but the closing date for applications is tomorrow. I wish I had seen the ad before. Now I'll have to act fast and get my résumé and cover letter together.

Umar: Does it say anything about the salary?

Sumalee: No. It just says the salary is negotiable. It can't be very high for someone fresh out of college. But I've found another ad which says that no experience is required. It's for an event and marketing trainee. A fixed salary comes with the job.

Umar: What qualities are they looking for?

Sumalee: It says: "Applicants must have good communication skills, be ambitious and able to work well under pressure. This is an entry-level marketing position. If you are not prepared to go through an intensive training program, please do not apply."

Well, I'm ambitious, I think my communication skills are good, and it's no problem for me to do a training program. I think I'll apply for that too. What about you, Umar? Have you found anything?

Umar: Yes, I have. Listen to this: "We are a large, international construction company in Kuala Lumpur. We are offering in-house training and permanent positions for junior office staff straight from college. We are looking for reliable, flexible team players who speak English and one other language. Closing date for applications: Friday, June 16. Please provide references."

Sumalee: Yes, that sounds like you – a reliable, flexible, team player who speaks English – and Malay too, of course. I'm sure our professor would give you a reference.

Umar: And I can get a second one from the boss of the travel agency I worked for during the summer vacation. She offered to give me one, but I didn't think I would need it. If only I hadn't said no.

Sumalee: That should be no problem. You have plenty of time before the closing date to call her and ask for one.

Umar: Yes, I think I'll do that right away.

Sumalee: And I'll start preparing my application for the fitness center job.

Umar: OK. See you later. Good luck!

Hello, my name is Helen Chu and I'm a management trainer. Part of my work is to help people to prepare for job interviews. I'm in touch with hiring managers in the human resources departments of several companies, and I've heard some horror stories from them. For example, there was the candidate who turned up late, chewing gum, and wearing old shorts and sandals. Or the telephone applicant whose call to one of the hiring managers ended suddenly. When the woman finally called back an hour later, she explained that she'd dropped her phone in the bathtub! And she didn't even apologize.

So here are my tips for avoiding mistakes when you're looking for a job.

Don't write a cover letter that repeats your résumé. The résumé contains all the details of your qualifications, skills, personal qualities, and experience. A cover letter should be short and precise and say something about what you can bring to the job. And, of course, have somebody check your résumé for grammar, spelling, and punctuation. Even one little mistake looks careless and can make a bad impression.

Doing poor research is another mistake. Before you go for an interview, find out as much as you can about the company – get on the Internet and find out its products or services, its history, size, and competitors. This will show the interviewers that you're really interested in their company. Write down some questions about the job and take your notebook with you to the interview. It makes you look professional and helps you to remember everything you wanted to ask.

Don't forget to clean up any social media pages you may have, such as Facebook or LinkedIn. Future employers don't need to see you in your bikini eating a big ice cream! Private pictures should be removed or locked down. Everyone, including college students, needs a professional LinkedIn profile.

During the interview be polite and friendly and make eye contact with the interviewers. Try not to move around too much in your chair as this will make you look nervous. Be positive about yourself and emphasize your strengths, but if the interviewers ask you about your weaknesses – a favorite question – just say one or two things and what you are doing to improve them.

That's all I want to tell you. If you remember my advice, you'll certainly be successful.

Track 44

Interviewer: Now, Kaori, I have your résumé here and I see you live in Osaka. Is that right?

Kaori: Yes, I live only a twenty-minute ride from here, so it's very convenient.

Interviewer: Yes, indeed. You studied web design at the Tokyo Design Technology Center. Tell me something about your course.

Kaori: Well, it was a two-year course and we learned not only the technical skills we needed to design websites and apps, but also the artistic side of web design. That was the part I liked most.

Interviewer: OK. I see that you have very little work experience.

Kaori: Well, I do have some. When I was studying in Tokyo, I worked part-time as a waitress at a sushi restaurant. When I left college, I had a three-month temporary job as an administrative assistant at GameZ, a video games company here in Osaka. I enjoyed that very much, but I was only standing in for somebody on maternity leave.

Interviewer: Now, you're a native Japanese speaker and you speak fluent English. Can you write English fluently?

Kaori: Oh, yes. My father is a businessman and when I was a child, we lived for six months in the United States. I went to school there.

Interviewer: So I'm sure you learned to write English too. And your technical skills must be excellent, of course. But, Kaori, you have had very, very little work experience, so what have you got to offer us?

Kaori: Well, I'm very willing to work hard and learn on the job. I'm also very flexible and can work well both independently and as part of a team.

Interviewer: And what attracts you to this company?

Kaori: Well, it seems to be a successful company, and the job you're offering is exactly what I'm looking for.

Interviewer: Can you provide references?

Kaori:	That's no problem. My college professor will be happy to give me a reference, and my boss at GameZ was very pleased with my work.
Interviewer:	Good. Then that's all for now. Let us have the references, Kaori, and you will hear from us soon. Thank you for coming.

Track 45

Conversation 1

Man:	Are you flying to Hawaii on vacation again this fall?
Woman:	No, I'm going to do something for the environment and fly to somewhere closer to home.
Man:	How does that help the environment?
Woman:	Because on average a flight from Chicago to Hawaii produces 1.08 metric tons of CO_2 and from Chicago to Florida only 0.3 metric tons.

Question 1 When will the woman take her vacation?

Question 2 Where is the woman going to spend her vacation?

Question 3 How much CO_2 will the woman's vacation flight produce?

Conversation 2

Woman:	I've read your résumé, but I'd like you to tell me something about yourself.
Man:	Yes, of course. Well, I was born here in New York, but I grew up in Tokyo. I studied international business at Kobe University.
Woman:	You know the job we're offering is in Osaka.
Man:	Yes. That's no problem for me. I speak fluent Japanese.
Woman:	And why do you want to work for our company?
Man:	Well, I saw your ad in a specialist journal, so I checked out your website and it seems to be an interesting place to work.

Question 1 Who is speaking?

Question 2 Where does the conversation take place?

Question 3 Where did the man see the ad?

Credits

The publisher would like to thank the following for permission to reproduce photographs and illustrations (key: left to right, top to bottom):